W9-BEN-884

Mother Teresa

Mother
Teresa

Maya Gold

DK PUBLISHING

LONDON, NEW YORK, MUNICH,
MELBOURNE, AND DELHI

Editor : Beth Hester
Publishing Director : Beth Sutinis
Designer : Mark Johnson Davies
Art Director : Dirk Kaufman
Photo Research : Anne Burns Images
Production : Ivor Parker
DTP Designer : Kathy Farias

First American Edition, 2008

08 09 10 11 12 10 9 8 7 6 5 4 3 2 1
Published in the United States
by DK Publishing
375 Hudson Street
New York, New York 10014

DK books are available at special discounts
when purchased in bulk for sales
promotions, premiums, fund-raising,
or educational use. For details, contact:

DK Publishing Special Markets
375 Hudson Street
New York, New York 10014
SpecialSales@dk.com

A catalog record for this book is available
from the Library of Congress.

ISBN 978-0-7566-3880-1 (Paperback)
ISBN 978-0-7566-3881-8 (Hardcover)

Printed and bound in China
by South China Printing Co., Ltd.

Photography credits:

Front Cover by Alamy/Tim Graham
Back Cover by by Dinodia

Discover more at
www.dk.com

Contents

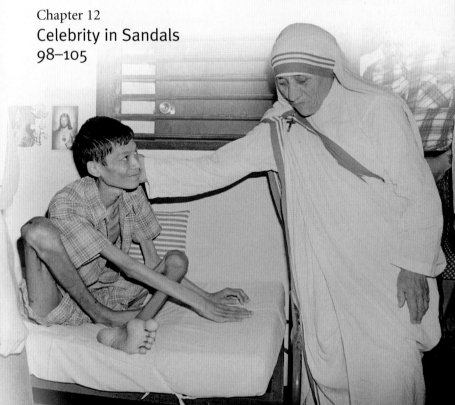

chapter 1

Little Bud

For most people, the words rich and famous are joined at the hip. It's hard to imagine a celebrity who left home at 18 to pursue a religious life, gave up all her worldly possessions except three identical outfits, a pair of sandals, and a tin washing pail, and chose to live and work among the poorest of the poor.

Yet Mother Teresa of Calcutta did just that, founding orphanages and shelters in her adopted home of India and around the globe. By the time of her death in 1997, she had gained thousands of followers working with needy, ill, and homeless people all over the world. She had met with many world leaders and won many honors, including the Nobel Peace Prize, which she accepted

Mother Teresa's radiant smile and simple garments made her a worldwide icon of charity.

in her sandals and plain cotton sari.

Who was this woman, and where did she come from? What inspired her to live her life in the way she did? How did someone who went out of her way to avoid the spotlight, calling herself "a little pencil in God's hands," become one of the most famous faces of the 20th century?

Agnes Gonxha Bojaxhiu was born on August 26, 1910, in the city of Skopje, now in the Republic of Macedonia. The baby girl's family called her Gonxha (pronounced gon-KHA), which means "little bud" or "flower bud" in Albanian. She had an older sister named Aga and an older brother named Lazar. Their father, Nikola Bojaxhiu, was a successful building contractor and merchant who traveled widely in Europe and even as far away as Egypt. Working with several partners, he traded in medicines and various luxury goods, including cloth, oil, sugar, and leather. Nikola, or "Kole," as his friends

Where Is Skopje?

Skopje lies within Macedonia, a small country just north of Greece. In this part of Europe, national boundaries have changed many times as different political groups came to power. At various times in history, Skopje was ruled by the Roman, Bulgarian, and Ottoman (Turkish) Empires. In modern times, it has been part of Serbia, Yugoslavia, and Albania.

7

called him, was a lively, handsome
man with a big mustache who
enjoyed giving gifts to his children
and telling them stories about his

travels to exotic lands. He also played in a brass band,
and was active in local arts and politics, financing the
construction of Skopje's first movie theater and serving on
the town council. He was of Albanian descent and spoke
five languages. Nikola was also fiercely nationalistic, and
supported the struggle for Albanian independence at a
time of great upheaval among neighboring nations.

In the years just before Agnes Gonxha was born, the
Ottoman Empire's centuries-old rule
of the region was starting to crumble,

Traditional peasant
garments in Skopje were
often decorated with
intricate patterns.

and ethnic Albanians hoped to create an independent nation. The Albanian National Movement was forcefully opposed by the Ottoman rulers, who punished its leaders harshly. Among other things, the Ottoman rulers insisted on using traditional Arabic script in place of the Latin alphabet favored by the Albanians—the alphabet we use in English today. The Bojaxhiu household was always full of men who came to talk to Nikola about politics and business, and

The graceful curves of Arabic script adorn richly decorated books and manuscripts.

many evenings included guests at the dinner table, long discussions of current events, and music, sometimes lasting late into the night.

Nikola's wife, Drana, was a traditional Albanian housewife who spent her days looking after the children, cooking, cleaning, and mending. Hardworking and strict, she was deeply religious, attending the Sacred Heart Church nearly every morning for Mass and supervising the family's evening prayers.

MASS
Mass is a Catholic religious ceremony or church service.

She was devoted to her husband, and no matter what chores she had been doing during the day, she always made sure that she and the children

were well dressed, clean, and ready to greet him when he came home for dinner.

The Bojaxhiu family was Roman Catholic, a minority religion in ethnically varied Skopje, where most people were Muslim or Orthodox Christian. There were also some Jews and a small population of Romanies, or Gypsies. Many languages were spoken, and the city's covered marketplace and cobblestone streets displayed a wide variety of pottery, textiles, and other handmade wares.

The long-tasseled red fez is traditional headgear for men of Turkish descent.

Muslim women wore veils in public, and some Skopje men wore Arabic robes or the traditional Turkish fez, a flat-topped red hat with a tassel. Some citizens wore the embroidered peasant costumes of the region, while other wore more modern European clothing. It was a rich and colorful brew of different cultures.

Since Catholics made up only about 10 percent of the Albanian population, Skopje's Catholic community was very close-knit. During religious holidays such as Easter and Corpus Christi, the Sacred Heart Church was decked with garlands of mountain flowers and cloth banners, with many candles burning inside the church. There were

PIETY

Piety is religious devotion and reverence. A pious person is one who obeys religious duties.

candlelit processions with young flower girls scattering rose petals and boys swinging incense lamps or carrying colored silk cloths over the heads of the priests.

Agnes and Aga both sang in the church choir, where they were known as "nightingales" because of their beautiful voices. This was remarkable, since Agnes was a delicate child who often suffered from coughs and weak lungs. Every year, the Bojaxhius made a pilgimage to the Church of the Madonna of Letnice, in the Black Mountains between Kosovo and Macedonia, near Skopje. They rode in a horse-drawn carriage, surrounded by pilgrims who prayed and sang as they made their way up the mountainside.

Even within this deeply religious community, Drana Bojaxhiu was known for her piety and

European religious processions often feature colorful costumes and pageantry.

generosity. She often gave money to needy strangers and sometimes invited them to join the family for meals or even to stay in their home. If a neighbor was sick, Drana would bring food and medicine and help nurse the invalid back to health. As a girl, Agnes often went with her mother on these visits, and came to see charitable giving as a moral and religious duty. Once, she accompanied her mother as she washed an elderly woman whose body was covered with sores. They also visited a mother of six who was dying, and helped to comfort and feed her family.

Drana made weekly visits to an alcoholic neighbor named File, and sometimes invited needy neighbors to join her family at the dinner table, where they were treated as welcomed guests.

As a girl, Agnes learned to play the mandolin, a wooden instrument with strings tuned in pairs.

These acts of kindness made a strong impression on her young daughter. So did Drana's insistence that charitable acts should never draw undue attention to the giver's own virtue. "When you do good, do it quietly, as if you were throwing a stone into the sea," she instructed her children, who sometimes called her Nana Loke, or "Mother of my Soul."

The Bojaxhius lived near the Vardar River, in a large house with a flower garden and fruit trees. Although girls

at that time were not always given an education, Nikola
sent all three of his children to school. They studied first
at a religious school run by the Sacred Heart Church and
later at public school, where they learned to speak and
write Serbo-Croatian as well as Albanian. Young Agnes
was studious, obedient, and rather serious, with big dark
eyes like her mother's, but she was not above helping her
brother Lazar with mischievous pranks, such as stealing
desserts from Drana's cupboard. Agnes also learned to
play the mandolin, sharing her father's love of singing and
music, and nurtured dreams of being a writer one day.

In later life, Mother Teresa spoke very little about her
early childhood and family life, saying only that it was
extremely happy. That happiness soon
would be tested by tragedy.

The Vardar River is spanned
by a massive stone bridge
many centuries old.

chapter 2

"Home Is Where the Mother Is"

When Agnes was still very young, central Europe was swept by a series of wars. The Balkan Wars fought by the countries surrounding her homeland were soon followed by the Great War (later called World War I), which was instigated in nearby Sarajevo.

Though Skopje was not at the center of the fighting, the upheavals shook the whole region. National boundaries were redrawn yet again, creating a new country that would later be called Yugoslavia. Many Albanian nationalists—including Nikola Bojaxhiu—felt that the Serbian province of Kosovo, where many Albanians lived, should belong to Albania, which had been independent since 1912.

Footsoldiers march past a mountain lake during World War I.

In 1919, Nikola traveled over 200 miles (350 km) to Belgrade, Yugoslavia, to attend a political dinner where these matters would be discussed. He was brought home in a carriage several days later, gravely ill. He was rushed straight to the hospital for emergency surgery, and Agnes was sent out to fetch a priest. Unable to find the priest of her family's own church, she went to the railroad station, where she spotted another priest on the train platform. He accompanied her to the hospital to give last rites to Nikola, who died within hours.

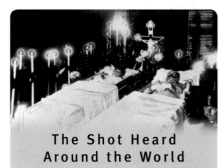

The Shot Heard Around the World

In 1914, Archduke Franz Ferdinand of Austria and his wife Sophie were shot by a Serbian assassin in Sarajevo. The killer was part of an underground group called the Black Hand (later aligned with Young Bosnia) dedicated to freeing Serbia from the Austro-Hungarian empire. This gunshot sparked a world war that stretched from 1914 to 1918, eventually involving much of Europe, as well as Russia and the United States.

Since he was just 45 years old and in good health, some of his relatives and even his doctors suspected he might have been poisoned because of his political leanings. This was never conclusively proved, but Lazar Bojaxhiu believed to the end of his days that his outspoken father

LAST RITES

Last rites are the prayers and rituals performed by a Catholic priest before someone's death.

15

had met with foul play. He and his sisters had learned a hard lesson about the courage it takes to stand up for one's beliefs.

Drana was devastated by her husband's death. Still reeling with grief, she soon learned that Nikola's Italian business partner had claimed all his properties and assets. She and her children still had a roof over their heads, but no source of income. It was a shocking blow, and for many months Drana was too severely depressed to manage the household. Most of the work fell to Aga, who was the oldest child at 15, but 8-year-old Agnes and 12-year-old Lazar felt the burden as well. Their mother had always been the unshakable head of their home, and it must have been frightening for her children to see her laid low by despair. It was also the first time they'd ever been faced with the kind of financial problems that faced their poorer neighbors.

But Drana had a resilient spirit, and the support of her faith and religious community. Tapping into the sewing skills she'd learned as a housewife, she started an embroidery business, at first selling her own handicrafts and eventually expanding her business to include other textiles and carpets. She also consulted with the managers of a local textile factory, offering them advice about which patterns, designs, and materials would be profitable. As soon as the hardworking widow and mother started earning enough money to take care of her family, she also resumed her charity visits. At one point, six orphaned children came to stay for a while in the family house. Drana was such a

strong inspiration to her daughter that Agnes would later say, "Home is where the mother is."

At the age of 12, Agnes felt strongly that she had been called to lead a religious life. She was deeply private about the details of this calling for the rest of her life, saying only that it didn't involve any vision or miracle. Nevertheless, she became convinced that religious service would be her path. She made pilgrimages on foot to the Church of the Madonna of Letnice in the Black Mountains, where she prayed alone, hoping to receive further guidance about how best to dedicate her life to her faith.

In 1925, when Agnes turned 15, a Jesuit priest named Father Franjo Jambrekovic became the new priest at the Sacred Heart Church. Father Jambrekovic was well-versed in science, medicine, arts, and

The Catholic Church

In the Middle Ages and after, the Christian church divided into a variety of branches, including Eastern Orthodoxy and Protestantism. Roman Catholicism, the largest branch, traces its roots back to Jesus' time. The Christian churches have much in common, but Catholicism is distinguished by its treatment of the sacraments, including Holy Communion and Confession; its missionary tradition; and its religious communities, called orders. Orders may include either women or men, but Catholic clergymen, called priests, are always unmarried men. Only a priest can lead Mass.

culture, and taught the young people of the parish about many of the things that interested him, including how to conduct an orchestra.

Energetic and inspiring, he offered concerts, walks, and other outings. He also started a library, where the studious Agnes spent long hours reading. Father Jambrekovic also formed a religious society for girls called the Sodality of the Blessed Virgin Mary. Agnes became an active member of this youth group, which introduced her to Saint Ignatius Loyola's *Spiritual Exercises,* which included such questions as "What have I done for Christ? What am I doing for Christ? What will I do for Christ?" She also taught religious classes to younger children, and discovered that she had a gift for teaching.

During this time, Father Jambrekovic told his young parishioners about a group of Jesuit missionaries who were working with the poor in Bengal, India. He shared magazine articles from *Catholic Missions* with the Sodality members. These articles included letters from the missionaries that vividly described the terrible living conditions in the communities they served.

Agnes was stirred by these reports, and by a visiting missionary who told the Sacred Heart congregation more about the Jesuits' mission in India and solicited donations. She even urged a cousin who earned extra money by giving

mandolin lessons to donate his earnings to the poor of India. Ever since she was very young, Agnes had dreamed of doing religious work in Africa or some other faraway place; now India became the place where she hoped to serve. By the age of 18, she had decided to become a missionary nun.

It wasn't an easy decision. Agnes was an excellent student with a strong interest in writing, especially poetry. She always carried a notebook in which she wrote down her thoughts, and had published two articles in a local newspaper. She was also a talented musician, and had thought about following a career in writing or music in addition to working with the church. Father Jambrekovic encouraged her to follow her heart, saying that if the thought of serving God and his people filled her with joy, it was the right path for her. He compared joy to a compass,

The Missionary Tradition

Many religious groups send missionaries into surrounding communities or remote places, where they hope to convert others to their beliefs. The missionary tradition exists among Mormons, Jehovah's Witnesses, Moravians, and Nichiren Shoshu Buddhists, to name just a few. Catholic missionaries take their inspiration from the words of Jesus: "Go therefore and make disciples of all nations: Baptize them . . . and teach them everything I have commanded you." (Matthew 28:19)

Nuns

A nun is a woman who takes vows committing herself to a religious life. Nuns also devote themselves to work such as teaching or serving the poor. They do not marry, though Catholic nuns call themselves "brides of Christ." The head of a community of nuns is known as the mother superior.

pointing the way to one's true vocation.

After much reflection and prayer, she decided to join the Sisters of Loreto, an Irish order that worked with the Jesuit brothers in Bengal, India. Finally, she would have a chance to see the places she'd heard so much about, and to make a difference in the lives of India's poor.

Although Drana had long suspected that Agnes would choose a religious vocation, she did not consent right away to her daughter's plans—possibly because she wanted to be sure of Agnes's determination. An often-repeated story claims that Drana went into her room, closed the door, and stayed there all day and night before giving Agnes her blessing, and urging her daughter to give herself over fully to God. When Lazar, who had already left home to become an Albanian military officer, questioned his sister's choice in a letter, Agnes replied, "You think

VOCATION

A vocation is a person's occupation, trade, or calling.

you are important because you are an officer serving a king with two million subjects. But I am serving the King of the whole world."

The Sodality group honored Agnes with a farewell concert at the church, and friends and family members came to the Bojaxhiu house afterward, bearing farewell gifts. Agnes was especially pleased to receive a gold fountain pen from her cousin—proof that her dreams of being a writer were far from over. For the rest of her life, she would continue to write, leaving an extensive legacy of letters, journals, and books.

Drana and Aga went with Agnes to the railroad station in Skopje. Agnes, who had never been far from her home before, waved her handkerchief and cried as friends and neighbors clustered to see her off. Her mother and sister traveled with her as far as Zagreb, Croatia, where Agnes bid them a difficult good-bye. She would never see either her mother or sister again.

In Zagreb, Agnes and Betika Kajnc, a young Yugoslavian woman who had also applied to join the Sisters of Loreto, boarded another train to Paris, where they would be interviewed by a French Mother Superior to determine their suitability for religious training. Agnes Gonxha Bojaxhiu was 18 years old, and about to begin a new life.

> *"I am serving the King of the whole world."*
>
> —Mother Teresa, in a letter to her brother

chapter 3

Sister of Loreto

The country where Agnes Gonxha and her new traveling companion, Betika, went to start their religious training was very different from the mountainous region around landlocked Skopje. Arriving on the "Emerald Isle" of Ireland, with its cool, misty climate and green, rolling hills, must have been both exciting and strange.

Although she had no way of knowing it at the time, the future Mother Teresa was joining a religious community akin to the one she would found in her later life. The Sisters of Loreto are affiliated with the Institute of the Blessed Virgin Mary (IBVM), which was founded by an Englishwoman named Mary Ward in 1609.

> **CLOISTER**
>
> A cloister is a place of religious seclusion, named for the covered walkway that many such buildings feature around their courtyards.

Ahead of her time in many ways, Ward believed that nuns should not live cloistered lives of prayer and meditation, but instead should carry

Christ's work out into the larger world to help the needy, much like the Jesuit brothers.

Ward also wanted her new order to be run by women, not just staffed by them—a radical idea in a time when women seldom held positions of leadership in any field, let alone in a church whose authority figures have always been men. It would be many years before church authorities recognized and accepted the IBVM.

The Loreto Sisters' convent was an imposing red brick and stone building in Dublin called Rathfarnham House. Agnes was comforted by the sight of a statue of the Blessed Virgin in its courtyard. Her religious faith, she knew, could travel across many nations. The two new arrivals spoke no English at all, and no one at

Agnes spent six weeks in training at the Sisters of Loreto convent in Rathfarnham House in Dublin, Ireland.

Rathfarnham spoke Albanian or Serbo-Croatian. English was an official language of Ireland and of India, which was then an English colony. In order to help the girls learn English faster, they were told never to speak to each other in their native tongues, an order that both obeyed dutifully.

Luckily, Agnes had inherited her father's gift for learning languages, and during her six-week training in Ireland she worked very hard at this task. Like the other postulants, she wore a long black dress called a habit and a black veil. By all accounts, she was quiet and hardworking, and adapted well to convent life in her short time at Rathfarnham. But her sights were set on India.

Christian missionaries had lived and worked in India for centuries. There was a small community of Christians in southern India dating back to Biblical times. In the 16th century, they were joined by Portuguese Catholics and the early Jesuits. The first Loreto Sisters mission to India was a group of seven nuns, two priests, and five postulants who sailed to Calcutta in 1841.

Nearly 90 years later, on December 1, 1928, postulants Agnes and Betika would board a ship called the *Marchait*, bound for India. They traveled from one exotic land to another, as their ship sailed across the Mediterranean Sea, through the Suez Canal to the Red Sea, and into the Indian Ocean and the Bay of Bengal. The voyage took five weeks, and the seas were often rough. Christmas came while they were at sea, and though there was no priest on board to celebrate Mass, three Franciscan nuns joined the girls to sing Christmas carols around a paper crib and stars.

At last the ship docked in Colombo, Ceylon (now Sri Lanka), a large island off the southern tip of India. The two young postulants were amazed by the sight of tall palm trees and tropical fruit, and by the crowded city with carts pulled not by horses but by sweating men in loincloths. Forced to ride in a rickshaw pulled by a very thin man, Agnes prayed that her weight would not be too much for him.

The passengers on the crossing from Colombo to Madras, India, included a Catholic priest. The postulant from Skopje who now called herself "Sister Mary Teresa of the Child Jesus" (soon to be shortened to "Sister Teresa") was happy to celebrate Mass once again. "Thanks be to God, we began the new year well with a sung Mass," she wrote.

Palm trees and brightly painted fishing boats were among the exotic sights on the coast of Ceylon.

chapter **4**

Darjeeling

The ship's first stop in India was the port city of Madras, where Sister Teresa was stunned by the "indescribable" poverty she witnessed. Although Skopje's population included many poor people, and ragged children sometimes begged for change in the marketplace, Sister Teresa had never seen anything like this. In an article for *Catholic Missions* magazine, she described whole families sleeping on the streets: "Day and night they live in the open on mats they have made from large palm leaves—or often on the

The overwhelming poverty in the streets of India had a huge impact on Sister Teresa.

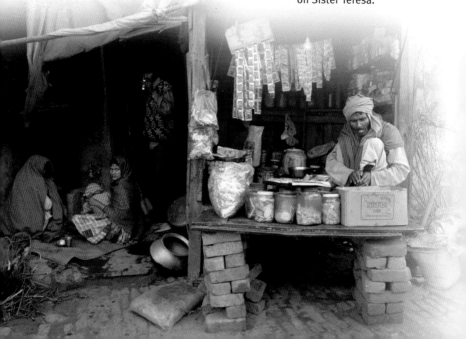

> *"If our people could only see all this, they would stop grumbling...and offer thanks to God ..."*
>
> –Mother Teresa

bare ground. They are all virtually naked, wearing at best a ragged loin cloth." She concluded: "If our people could only see all this, they would stop grumbling about their own misfortunes and offer thanks to God for blessing them with such abundance."

The southern part of India is very close to the equator, and for someone accustomed to snow at Christmastime, the tropical heat and relentless bright sun was hard to take. India is also a feast of color. The city of Madras was crowded with brightly painted carts and wooden rickshaws, women wearing saris of orange and peacock blue, and humpbacked cattle wandering loose in the streets.

The sounds of unfamiliar languages and

"Champagne of Teas"

The name "Darjeeling" is known around the world for the rich, flavorful tea that comes from this region. Tea is a drink with a long and colorful history; its popularity influenced exploration and trade for centuries. In the 15th and 16th centuries, Europe's demand for tea and spices prompted naval explorations by Christopher Columbus and Vasco Da Gama. And in 1600, the British East India Company was founded by royal charter to promote trade in Indian goods, especially tea and spices. The company became a colonial power; in the 1700s, the East India Company even had its own military department.

27

The snow-covered Himalayas are a breathtaking backdrop to Darjeeling's hills. Kachenjunga, at right, is the third highest peak in the world.

musical chanting, the scents of jasmine blossoms and spicy foods fried by street vendors must have seemed otherworldly.

After a short stay in Madras, the ship continued sailing up India's eastern coast to its final destination, Calcutta. This larger, poorer, and infinitely more overwhelming city would be home to Mother Teresa for the greater part of her life. But this first visit was brief. In a matter of days, she was sent to the Sisters of Loreto's convent in Darjeeling to complete her training.

HILL STATION

Hill stations are Indian towns at elevations of 3,500–7,500 ft (1000–1500 m), often used as cool retreats from the summer heat.

The town of Darjeeling sits in the foothills of the Himalayas, the tallest mountain range on Earth. Local legend holds that the snow-capped

Himalayas are the sacred resting place of the Hindu god Shiva. The name Darjeeling comes from the Tibetan words

dorje (thunderbolt) and *ling* (dwelling place). Together, they mean "land of the thunderbolt." Darjeeling enjoyed cool mountain air, a good climate, and breathtaking views, making it a popular "hill station" and resort for British colonials and wealthy Indians during the summer months, when the heat and humidity of the coastal cities was too much to bear.

The 400-mile (700-km) train trip to Darjeeling was very dramatic. The Darjeeling Himalayan Railway climbs

The British Raj in India

The United Kingdom consists of England, Scotland, Northern Ireland, and Wales, which occupy two islands in the north Atlantic. But for centuries, the British Empire extended much farther. The British, avid explorers and seafarers, claimed colonies on many continents, including North America, Australia, Africa, as well as "the jewel in the crown," India. The British rule of India from 1858–1947 was called the *Raj* (the Indian word for "reign").

thousands of feet in elevation, laboring up steep slopes and around tight spiraling curves, one of which is called "Agony Point." Most of the Darjeeling district is more than a mile above sea level, and its steep hillsides are ideal for growing one of India's most important crops, tea.

In this picturesque region of lush tea plantations and snow-capped peaks, the Loreto Convent was a world apart. Behind its stone walls, the nuns and novices followed a rigorous schedule of daily study and prayers, rising early and working hard all day long. Their training was closely supervised by the novice mistress, who was charged with evaluating their work. Sister Teresa was known for her tireless and cheerful disposition,

Workers harvest the famed Darjeeling tea, sometimes known as "the champagne of teas."

but she was not good at everything. One of her teachers would later recall her clumsiness at lighting the tall candles in the chapel. She continued to study English, and also learned two of India's major languages: Bengali and Hindi.

Every morning, Sister Teresa and the other novices taught local students at St. Teresa's school, a one-room schoolhouse serving about 20 girls and boys. She was well liked by her young students, who nicknamed her "Ma" (mother) and "Bengali Teresa" because of her ease and fluency in that language. She was also assigned to work for a short time with the nursing staff of a nearby medical station, and her contact with the desperate, ill, and sometimes starving people—many of whom had walked for hours to get help—made a lasting impression on her. So did a painting of Jesus surrounded by sufferers that hung on the hospital pharmacy's wall. She wrote

India's Many Languages

Indians speak hundreds of different languages, ranging from the official language of Hindi to dialects spoken in only a handful of villages. A 2001 census identified 22 languages that were spoken by over a million people, including Bengali and Punjabi in the north, Marathi in central and western India, and Tamil and other Dravidian languages in the south. To make matters even more complicated, many Indian languages have their own scripts and alphabets. English is also a recognized and common language.

in *Catholic Missions,* "Each morning, before I start work, I look at this picture. In it is concentrated everything that I feel. I think, 'Jesus, it is for you and for these souls!' Then I open the door."

On May 24, 1931, Agnes Gonxha Bojaxhiu took her first vows in the convent's chapel, pledging herself to a life of poverty, chastity, and obedience to God. At that time, the ceremony included prostration, or lying face-down on the floor, a symbolic death of the postulant's former life and worldly desires. When she got up, she had become a new person, embarked on a lifelong vocation of religious service. The tradition of her religious order also dictated that she must now confirm the new name she had chosen for herself in Ireland.

Though not all orders require members to change their names, this practice is common in

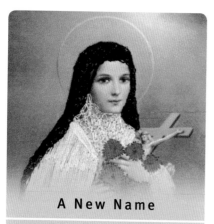

A New Name

Agnes Gonxha chose her new name to honor Saint Thérèse of Lisieux, a humble French nun who lived a quiet life of prayer and died at the tender age of 24. Her nickname was "Little Flower"—an appropriate choice for the "little bud" Gonxha, who stood barely over five feet (1.5 m) tall. Since another nun at the Darjeeling convent already bore the French name Marie-Therese, Agnes Gonxha adopted the Spanish spelling Teresa instead.

Roman Catholicism and other religious faiths. To symbolize the start of a new life, a person leaves behind his or her birthname, and instead chooses a name with some special meaning or

"Each morning, before I start work, I look at this picture. . . . I think, 'Jesus, it is for you and for these souls!"

–Mother Teresa

tradition. Since the Middle Ages, popes have chosen new names upon taking office, often in honor of former popes or favorite saints. In some forms of Buddhism, high-ranking religious teachers choose spiritual names (sometimes called Dharma names) for their students. It is also common for a person to take a new name when converting to a different religion, as demonstrated by the boxer Muhammad Ali (formerly Cassius Clay) and the basketball player Kareem Abdul-Jabbar (formerly Lew Alcindor), both of whom changed their names when they converted to the religion of Islam.

Not long after she took her first vows, Sister Teresa was reassigned to teach at St. Mary's, a convent school run by the Sisters of Loreto in Calcutta. This would be her home for nearly two decades. For the second time, she boarded the Darjeeling Himalayan Railway train. This time, however, she was traveling away from the peace and beauty of the Darjeeling hills and heading toward poor and troubled Calcutta, soon to be her new home.

chapter 5

India in Transition

Although Sister Teresa had spent a few days in Calcutta when she first arrived in India, moving there from Darjeeling was a shocking transition. Far from being a breezy mountain resort town, India's third largest city was hot, humid, and desperately overcrowded. Its slums were lined with makeshift tin and cardboard shacks, and many beggars lived right on the streets and sidewalks. Indian-born English writer Rudyard Kipling, author of *The Jungle Book*, called it the "City of Dreadful Night."

Beggars are a common sight on the streets of Calcutta.

There were other sides to Calcutta as well. Once called "the City of Palaces," it had been the capital of the British Raj until 1911. Some neighborhoods were prosperous, with elegant Victorian architecture and a healthy cultural life, while others were known for their racy nightclubs and prostitutes. But the Sisters of Loreto convent

at Entally, a complex of several buildings, green lawns, and athletic fields enclosed by high walls, was next to one of the city's poorest slums, known as *Moti Jihl,* or "Pearl Lake." (The name referred to a discolored pond at its center.) Though the Loreto Sisters almost never left their walled compound because of their order's strict rules of enclosure, the sights Sister Teresa had seen just outside its wrought-iron gates were etched deeply in her heart and mind.

The Black Hole of Calcutta

Calcutta was notorious for an incident in 1756, in which more than 100 British civilians and soldiers were jailed overnight in a dungeon so tiny and airless that most of them were smothered to death by morning. Though some historians now doubt these reports, the phrase "Black Hole of Calcutta" lodged in the public imagination, adding to the city's dark reputation.

During her many years at Loreto Entally, Sister Teresa was known as a dedicated and cheerful worker. Rising at 5:00 every morning, she prayed and studied before going to Mass in the chapel. At St. Mary's School (one of two in the Entally complex), she worked side by side with Bengali nuns from a different order, who wore simple traditional saris in white or blue in place of the Loreto Sisters' full-length black-and-white habits. By all accounts, Sister Teresa was a gifted teacher who brought her geography and history lessons to life for the young students of St. Mary's School. In her geography classes, she told stories about growing up in Skopje, and had a talent for describing even those places

The Caste System

India has a rigid system of castes or social classes. Traditionally, the caste a person is born into determines what kind of work he or she may do. *Brahmans* are priests, scholars, and teachers. *Kshatriyas* are rulers and warriors. *Vaishyas* are merchants and farmers. *Sudras* are manual laborers. *Dalits* ("Untouchables") are outcasts. Today, changes in economic or political status may allow people to overcome the limitations of their castes, especially in modern cities.

she'd never seen firsthand in vivid detail. The sisters taught in a variety of spaces, including a former chapel that had been divided into five classrooms, a former stable, and sometimes outside in the courtyard.

The Loreto schools in Entally had an excellent reputation, educating "Loreto girls" who often went on to college and became educators and social workers. Together, the two schools in Entally served about 500 girls, a mixture of well-to-do Indians, children of foreigners who were living in India, and local orphans who lived at the school. All wore the same uniform to erase the difference between their backgrounds, but this was not easy in class-conscious India.

Every day, before she started class, Sister Teresa washed and swept the floor of her classroom. This was a source of great fascination for her Indian students, since such chores were always performed

"Do not forget that you went to India for the sake of the poor."

—Drana Bojaxhiu

by servants from the lower castes, not by professionals such as teachers. Among other duties, Sister Teresa supervised the children's recreation hour and oversaw the evening meals and bedtime routine of the students who boarded at the school. She also made sure that the local children who came to St. Mary's School received regular baths, a great treat for many who lived without plumbing at home. Sister Teresa was firm about following the rules, but rarely lost her temper with her students. She expected them to treat each other with kindness, and was always ready to offer a smile or hold a child's hand.

A handleless broom, made by binding together a bunch of twigs or dried grasses, is frequently used for sweeping by lower-caste Indians.

Sister Teresa taught at St. Mary's School for many years, and was eventually asked to become its headmistress. When she wrote to her mother about this achievement, Drana sent back a stern letter, reminding her daughter of her vocation: "Dear child, Do not forget that you went to India for the sake of the poor."

In addition to her teaching duties, Sister Teresa helped organize the school's chapter of the Sodality of the Blessed Virgin, the same youth group she had joined back in Skopje. Though some of the boarding students went out once a week with a Jesuit priest, Father Julien Henry, to visit hospitals and poor

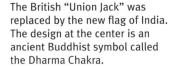

The British "Union Jack" was replaced by the new flag of India. The design at the center is an ancient Buddhist symbol called the Dharma Chakra.

families in Moti Jihl, Sister Teresa was forbidden by convent rules to accompany them. This must have weighed on her mind as she taught the children of well-to-do families inside the convent, while those she most wanted to serve lived just outside its walls.

She did leave the Entally convent a few times during these years, most notably in May 1937, when she traveled once more to Darjeeling to take her final vows, changing her name for the last time. Now 26 years old, she would be known for the rest of her life by the name Mother Teresa.

There had been many changes in India during Mother Teresa's long years of seclusion. The Indian people had grown increasingly dissatisfied with their colonial status, and a movement for independence, or home rule, was growing in strength. At its forefront was Mohandas K. Gandhi, a small man of unshakable convictions whose followers called him "Mahatma," or Great Soul.

India's resentment of the British Raj became even stronger in 1939, when England's parliament declared a

state of war with Nazi Germany. Just as they had done during World War I, the British dragged their colonies into World War II without asking for their consent. Since the British empire was vast, with outposts in Africa, the Middle East, parts of Indochina, and India, the term "world war" was painfully accurate. England's allies France and Belgium were also colonial powers with extensive holdings on other continents, further expanding the scope of the fighting.

Calcutta was the center of British military operations in India and other parts of Asia during World War II, and there was a constant threat of air raids from the enemy nation of Japan. During the war, all transportation systems in India, from national railroads to the riverboats used to deliver rice, were taken over by the British military. Shipments of rice from neighboring Burma were stopped altogether. These shortages

Gandhi and the Indian Independence Movement

Born in 1869, Gandhi trained as a lawyer in England and went to work in South Africa. His experiences with racial discrimination led him to establish a new form of social activism called nonviolent resistance, or *satyagraha*. Through mass demonstrations and symbolic acts, such as leading a march to the coast to harvest sea salt rather than paying the English salt tax, he galvanized India's quest for home rule.

combined with two winter-harvest disasters—a cyclone and a flood—to cause the Great Famine of 1943.

It is estimated that two to four million Indians died of hunger during this time. Calcutta's teeming streets were swelled by hundred of thousands of starving villagers, and the war refugees who were flooding into a city whose meager resources and soup kitchens were already strained beyond measure. Beggars slept in railway stations or lay starving on the sidewalks.

The Loreto Sisters at Entally were directly affected by the famine and the war. Food for the students and nuns was now in short supply, and war-orphaned babies were frequently left at their doorstep. At one point, Mother Teresa and her peers were caring for 24 babies at once. Catholic missionaries who had escaped from Japan asked for shelter along with other war refugees. Then British military commanders took over the convent buildings, converting the schools and orphanage into a hospital

War on Many Continents

War broke out between Japan and China in 1937, and in 1939, Germany invaded Poland and other countries in Europe. When France, Belgium, and England entered the war with their colonies, much of the world was divided between the Allies of Western Europe (joined by Australia and the United States) and the Axis led by Germany, Japan, and Italy. By the time the war ended in 1945, more than 70 million people had died.

complex for sick and wounded soldiers. The Loreto Sisters—
along with the boarding students and orphans in their
charge—were forced to relocate. Some were sent away to
Darjeeling and to convents in other cities, but Mother Teresa
was able to continue teaching in a building on Calcutta's
Convent Road.

After the war ended in 1945, the Loreto Sisters returned
to their home at Entally. But the world outside their gates
was still far from peaceful. As the movement for Indian
independence grew, so did the tension between the country's
two major religious groups. Muslims feared that an
independent India ruled by the Hindu
majority would exclude them even more

A poor Indian tends a
cooking fire on the streets of
a slum neighborhood near
the Calcutta railway station.

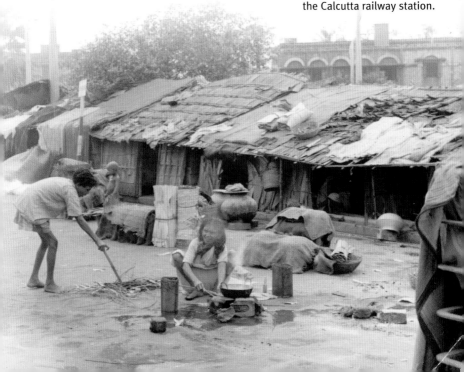

forcefully than the British Raj. They pressed for partition into two independent countries, one Hindu and one Muslim.

On a brutally hot August day in 1946, these tensions erupted into violent riots in the streets of Calcutta, in what became known as the Direct Action Day, or the Day of Great Killing. More than 5,000 people were killed and thousands more wounded, and soldiers were called in to stop the rioting. The city's services ground to a halt, and with all food deliveries suspended, Mother Teresa went into the streets alone to get food for the 300 students who boarded at Entally. What she witnessed horrified her: "I saw bodies in the street, stabbed, beaten, lying there in dried blood." She

Calcutta police sometimes used tear-gas bombs to quell violent rioting.

was stopped on the street by uniformed soldiers, who drove her back to the school with a truckload of rice for her hungry students. For many weeks afterward, the city was filled with smoke as the piles of bodies were burned in accordance with Hindu ritual.

It was during these difficult years that Mother Teresa met Father Celeste Van Exem, a Belgian Jesuit who would become her lifelong spiritual advisor and close confidant. At first, they seemed to make an unlikely pair. Father Van Exem was an expert in the Arabic language and Muslim religious traditions, who had lived for several years among Bedouin Arabs. A bookish and scholarly man, he would later admit that he was less than enthusiastic when his superiors assigned him to advise the young Mother Teresa, a pious and simple nun who had a deep interest in helping the poor, but had led a sheltered existence within convent walls. This would soon change, as Father Van Exem came to sense something extraordinary in this humble nun.

> ### India's Many Religions
>
> India is a deeply religious country, with statues, shrines, and temples visible everywhere. The majority religion is Hinduism, founded about 5,000 years ago. Hindus believe in many gods and goddesses, and the cycles of birth, life, death, and reincarnation (called *samsara*). The largest minority religion is Islam, founded in the seventh century by the Arab prophet Muhammad. Followers of Islam, called Muslims, believe in one god (*Allah* in Arabic). There are also Sikhs, Buddhists, Jains, and small populations of Zoroastrians, Christians, and Jews in India.

6

The Call Within a Call

Mother Teresa's health had been frail since childhood, and the stresses of dealing with so many wartime crises had weakened her even further. In the weeks following the Day of Great Killing, she became so ill that her supervisors were afraid she might fall victim to tuberculosis, a lung disease that had claimed many lives in Calcutta. When a doctor insisted that she stop working so hard and spend at least three hours a day in bed, she wept with frustration. Father Van Exem would later remember this as the only time he ever saw Mother Teresa cry. Her supervisors decided that she should return

The train journey to Darjeeling includes many tight loops and steep inclines.

to the convent in Darjeeling for a period of rest and meditation.

Mother Teresa left Calcutta for her relaxing retreat. But

during the familiar ride on the Darjeeling Himalayan Railway, something happened that would change her life forever. Over the noise of the rattling train, Mother Teresa heard the voice of God. "I was sure it was God's voice," she would later tell Father Julien Henry. "I was certain that He was calling me. The message was clear: I must leave the convent to help the poor by living among them. This was a command, something to be done, something definite. I knew where I had to be. But I did not know how to get there." As with her first call from God at age 12, Mother Teresa considered this to be an extremely personal experience and said very little about it to others, comparing the call to a hidden treasure.

Mother Teresa knew well that the Catholic Church had strict regulations governing its nuns' activities, and that leaving the convent to work with the poor would not be an option unless she received special permission from church authorities. During her retreat in Darjeeling, she prayed fervently for further guidance. When she returned to Calcutta, she met with Father Van Exem

Inspiration Day

The date of Mother Teresa's "call within a call," September 10, 1946, is known as Inspiration Day. It is celebrated worldwide every year by members of the order she founded, the Missionaries of Charity.

45

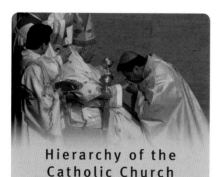

Hierarchy of the Catholic Church

A hierarchy is a system of ranking people or things in a specific order. Catholic clergymen follow a specific hierachy, with the chain of power rising from priest to bishop to archbishop to cardinal and finally to the pope, the highest authority in the church. The word "pope" comes from the Italian word *papa*, or father.

and told him about the experience she described as "the call within a call"—she had been called by God once to become a nun, and now felt herself called to move outside the rules by which all nuns lived. She wanted to found a new order whose members would live and work not in a cloistered community, but among the poor they served. She gave him two sheets of paper, on which she had written down her plans. They outlined most of the basic precepts for the order she would eventually lead, including a focus on those who were abandoned, unwanted, or without any family. The members of Mother Teresa's new order would take a special vow of charity for the poor, whom they would serve in a spirit of poverty and cheerfulness without the help of hospitals or other institutions.

Father Van Exem listened with his customary sympathy. He would later say that he never doubted the

ARCHDIOCESE

An archdiocese is the district and population supervised by an archbishop. Dioceses, supervised by bishops, are made up of parishes.

authenticity of her call, explaining, "Mother was not an exceptional person. She was an ordinary Loreto nun, a very ordinary person but with great love for her Lord." This very ordinariness, he felt, was proof

that this extraordinary call had come directly from God. He advised Mother Teresa to write to the mother general (head of the order) of the Loreto Sisters, asking permission to contact the governing bodies in Vatican City and to be released from her teaching duties at Loreto Entally. He also suggested that she meet with the head of the Calcutta archdiocese, Archbishop Ferdinand Périer.

Mother Gertrude M. Kennedy, mother general of the Loreto Sisters, sent her wholehearted approval. "Since this is manifestly the will of God, I give you permission to write to the Congregation in Rome," she wrote, adding that Mother Teresa should "tell nobody" of her unconventional plans. But Archbishop Périer was unconvinced. When he heard that "a young nun of the Community had some queer ideas," he was troubled by the prospect of a lone European-born nun roaming the slums of Calcutta. He also worried about how releasing Mother Teresa from her convent obligations would affect others at Loreto Entally. He decided to postpone the decision for a year.

In the meantime, Mother Teresa was assigned to teach geography and manage the kitchen and garden of a convent in Asansol, a mining town over one hundred miles (161 km) northwest of Calcutta. From the hills of Asansol, she wrote many beautiful and poetic letters to Father Van Exem, about both her spiritual path and the flowers she tended in the convent gardens.

During this time, Archbishop Périer met with other church authorities. Without revealing Mother Teresa's identity, he discussed her proposal with Father Julien Henry, who supported the idea with enthusiasm and asked his congregation to pray for the "Mother of the Poor." The archbishop also consulted the father general of the Jesuit order, and a specialist in church law.

Eventually Archbishop Périer agreed to allow Mother Teresa to write to the Vatican requesting special permission to leave the convent. However, he stipulated that she must ask for permission not only to leave the convent, but also to give up her vows as a nun.

Vatican City's Piazza San Pietro was designed by the 17th century architect Gian Lorenzo Bernini.

Although she was convinced that she must separate herself from the

Sisters of Loreto, Mother Teresa was determined to remain bound to Jesus. Still, she never wavered from her conviction that this was what God had told her to do. She agreed to the terms of the archbishop's letter, and prayed for a positive outcome.

Pope Pius XII was head of the Catholic church in Vatican City at the time of Mother Teresa's "call within a call."

It would be a long wait. The letter was sent in February 1948, and no reply came until July. When Father Van Exem told Mother Teresa that he had received word from Rome, she turned pale and went into the chapel to pray before hearing the news. When she learned that she had received special permission to leave the convent for a year without renouncing her vows, Mother Teresa was thrilled beyond measure. She signed all three copies of the letter, then turned to Father Van Exem and asked, "Can I go to the slums now?"

chapter **7**

Outside Convent Walls

Many years later, Mother Teresa would tell an interviewer that leaving the convent was the hardest thing she had ever done, even more wrenching than leaving home when she was young. When she left her family, she had put herself in the hands of the church to pursue her calling, as thousands of young women had done before her. She had entered an orderly world where all decisions were made for her by her religious superiors, and her only job was to obey

Saris

The traditional Hindu garment for women, called a sari or saree, has been worn for thousands of years. It consists of a rectangular strip of unstitched cloth, 42–49 in (106–124 cm) wide and 5–9 yards (94.6–8.2 m) long, which is draped around the body in a variety of styles, usually around the waist and over one shoulder, sometimes also over the top of the head. Most women wear a petticoat and a *choli*, or short blouse, underneath. Woven of silk or cotton, saris often have patterned edges, and some are elaborately embroidered.

with a cheerful heart. Now, she was taking a giant leap into the unknown, armed only with her conviction that God had chosen this path for

> *"We young ones . . . couldn't fathom her leaving."*
>
> —Sister Marie Thérèse

her. It must have taken tremendous courage and discipline.

The Loreto Sisters at Entally were stunned to find out that Mother Teresa was leaving them. One sister named Mother Cenacle cried uncontrollably, and the mother superior was so overcome with emotion that she took to her bed for a week. The nuns were a close-knit community, and they had taken it for granted that they would live and work together for the rest of their lives. They were also concerned for Mother Teresa's safety if she followed her plan to go live in the slums, and also for her fragile health. Many of the sisters could not understand why she would abandon the convent where she'd seemed so happy. "We young ones essentially couldn't fathom her leaving," Sister Marie Thérèse later recalled. But nothing could change Mother Teresa's determination. A notice was posted on the blackboard with words of advice for the Loreto Sisters: "Do not criticize. Do not praise. Pray."

In preparation for her new life, Mother Teresa went to a local bazaar and bought three simple white cotton saris, each with three blue stripes at the edge.

BAZAAR

A bazaar is a marketplace, often outdoors or under a simple roof, containing many small stalls or shops.

It is hard to imagine how strange the simple activity of going to a market to buy new clothes must have seemed to someone who had dressed for two decades in the simple black-and-white garments provided for her by her order. Imagine the sights, sounds, and smells of an open-air bazaar in an Indian city: Farmers place cloths on the ground, selling bright-colored peppers, eggplants, and okra, or live chickens in slatted cages. Vendors squat next to flat baskets heaped with fragrant spices, dried chickpeas, and lentils. Women in saris display shiny bangles and nose rings, and dark-eyed girls string wedding garlands of orange marigold blossoms. On a makeshift charcoal stove, someone fries flat breads stuffed with onions, and the pungent aromas of curry and smoke fill the air.

Indian bazaars, such as this open-air flower market, are a swirl of color and bustling activity.

Nuns' Habits

The loose, long garments traditionally worn by Catholic nuns are called habits. They can include several pieces: a tunic dress, a white coif around the face, and a veil and underveil over the head. Some orders add such pieces as a stiff white crown band around the forehead, a biblike wimple, a short cape called a capuche, or an overlayer called a scapular. These may be black, white, or other solid colors. Each order has a distinctive habit, and within the order, different colors may be worn by novices and nuns. Modern nuns often wear modified habits or simple street clothes.

The simple saris that Mother Teresa chose were the cheapest kind available, usually worn by peasant women who couldn't afford finer garments. The blue stripes appealed to her because blue is the color traditionally associated with the Virgin Mary. Father Van Exem performed a special blessing on her new garments, and added a small cross at the shoulder and rosary beads. This uniform has been worn by Missionaries of Charity ever since, in all climates and continents, sometimes with the addition of a cardigan sweater or simple cloth coat in cold weather. The standard footwear is a simple pair of sandals.

On August 16, 1948, Mother Teresa went to her room in the convent for the last time and removed the long black habit and veil she had worn for so many years.

In its place, she put on one of the white cotton saris, draping it over her head and around her body. Having lived in a convent for so long, she had few possessions apart from her two other saris, her notebook, and a pen. Although some of Mother Teresa's students hoped they would get to see their teacher dressed in a sari, she left very quietly at night, bringing only a few rupees and a train ticket to Patna, an ancient city on the Ganges River.

The Ganges, considered by Hindus to be a sacred entity, is joined by three other rivers near Patna, where its waters are exceptionally wide. Patna is a pilgrimage site for Sikhs and Buddhists as well as Hindus, and also a thriving business center and the capital of the state of Bihar.

A rosary is a string of beads with a crucifix attached, used by Roman Catholics for counting prayers.

Before Mother Teresa started her work in Calcutta, Father Van Exem had arranged for her to spend several months in Patna, training with the Medical Mission Sisters at the Holy Family Hospital. The sisters were mostly European and American women who had trained as doctors, midwives, and other medical professionals, and now taught nursing skills and nutrition basics to Indian women, including some former Loreto girls. At the hospital, Mother Teresa learned how to attend to patients dying of smallpox and cholera, how to give injections, make beds with hospital corners, and assist in delivering babies. At first, she was anxious about handling newborns, afraid she would damage their delicate bodies, but she soon came to love working with babies. She was also especially good at soothing small children who were

Trading her nun's habit for a white cotton sari and sandals was a groundbreaking choice for Mother Teresa.

scared of the hospital, and at comforting the dying. One of the medical sisters who served with her commented that Mother Teresa always managed to remain calm in a crisis.

She also learned about the importance of proper nutrition. She had originally planned for her order to live on a humble diet of nothing but rice and salt, as many poor

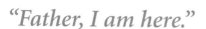

"Father, I am here."

— Mother Teresa

Indians did, but Mother Dengel, the founding mother of the Medical Mission Sisters, convinced Mother Teresa that she and her followers would become too weak to carry out their work if they did not also include some protein, fruit, and vegetables in their simple meals, and make sure to get enough rest. Mother Dengel suggested that they conclude their day's activities, household chores, and prayers by 9:00 PM and schedule one day of rest every week to maintain their strength. Their saris should be washed every day. Otherwise, the nuns would be likely to catch the same diseases they were trying to treat among their poor patients.

Although her days were full of prayer and hospital duties, Mother Teresa spent her evenings working on plans for her new order's daily schedule and rules. In the Patna convent's simple sleeping cubicles, divided from each other by a system of bamboo rods and cotton sheets, she took notes and made lists, growing impatient to start her new life. Within a few weeks, she had written to Father Van Exem, requesting that she be allowed to return to Calcutta immediately. She felt she had learned all she needed from the Holy Family Hospital; the rest, she would surely be able to learn as she worked among the poor. Both Father Van Exem and the archbishop were skeptical. They had expected Mother Teresa to stay in Patna for six months

to a year. Father Van Exem tried to impress upon her the importance of adequate medical training, but her letters kept coming, making the same request. At last, he agreed to come see her in Patna to discuss the matter further. When he arrived at the hospital, he did not recognize Mother Teresa among the sari-clad nurses until she said, "But Father, I am here." Eventually, the Medical Mission Sisters helped convince Father Van Exem that Mother Teresa had picked up the basics of nursing and was ready to start her work in the slums.

Not long after that, Mother Teresa was granted permission to move back to Calcutta, where she would go into the streets by herself and begin a new kind of mission.

The city of Patna, where Mother Teresa studied nursing, is home to the Patna Sahib Gurudwara, a sacred pilgrimage site for Sikhs.

The Poorest of the Poor

The Calcutta that Mother Teresa was going to serve was more needy than ever. Just a year earlier, India had finally won independence from the British Empire, but at a cruel price. The rift between Muslim and Hindu leaders had grown so deep that the former colony was split into two different countries: a Hindu India, and a Muslim Pakistan. The island of Ceylon (Sri Lanka) became its own country as well.

For centuries, Hindus and Muslims had lived side by side, so with Partition came one of the largest migrations of refugees in human history. Many Muslims who had been living in India fled with their families to the new nation of Pakistan, which had been carved out in two

A Nation Divided

The division of the former British colony of India was known as Partition. Gandhi, who had spent his life working toward a free India and peace among peoples of different religions and ethnic groups, was heartbroken by Partition. He refused to lead a divided India, and his long-term colleague Jawaharlal Nehru became its first prime minister.

sections, to the east and west of India. Meanwhile, many Hindu families who had lived in the areas that were now part of Pakistan

fled into India. In all, over 16 million people moved between the two countries, mostly by foot, and there was much bloodshed along the new borders. Former neighbors now saw each other as enemies, and many were killed before they ever reached their new homes.

Now 78 years old, Gandhi went on a fast to protest the violence between Muslims and Hindus, refusing to eat until there was peace in the streets. "I am prepared to die," he once said, "but there is no cause for which I am prepared to kill." Gandhi was so beloved by the Indian people that the rioting stopped. He agreed to stop fasting, but just two weeks later, on January 30, 1948, he was shot by a Hindu

A stream of refugees moved between India and Pakistan, carrying all their possessions on foot or in carts.

assassin. All of India mourned Gandhi's death. More than one million people attended his funeral.

Calcutta was the closest major Indian city to East Pakistan, and during Partition, huge numbers of Hindu refugees moved there looking for food, jobs, and places to live. Remember that the population of Calcutta—already a poor and overcrowded city—had recently been swollen by many thousands of famine victims seeking shelter. Now there were thousands more homeless refugees, most without any possessions except for the clothes on their backs. This made Mother

Calcutta's slums were full of hastily constructed shacks.

Teresa's mission among the poor even more urgent.

Father Van Exem arranged for Mother Teresa to live with an order called the Little Sisters of the Poor, who ran a nursing home for the poor and aged called St. Joseph's Home for the Elderly. The Little Sisters lived a simple life of poverty, depending on donations of food and money. They drew inspiration from the words of their founder, Jeanne Jugan: "It is so good to be poor, to have nothing, to depend on God for everything." This would become an important principle of Mother Teresa's new order as well. Its members would own next to nothing, and their care would be up to the grace of God and the charity of their neighbors.

"It is so good . . . to depend on God for everything."

—Jeanne Jugan, founder of the Little Sisters of the Poor

On December 21, 1948, Mother Teresa dressed in her white-and-blue cotton sari and a pair of rough sandals the Patna sisters had given her. She left St. Joseph's Home and went to morning Mass in a neighboring church. Then she boarded a bus that would take her to the infamous slum neighborhood of Moti Jihl, near Loreto Entally.

Calcutta's slums were a jumble of shacks and huts made out of anything people could get their hands on: mud bricks, flattened cardboard boxes, hammered tin cans, sheets of corrugated metal, or plastic. Even though most of these dwellings had dirt floors and makeshift roofs, landlords charged rent to their occupants. Those who couldn't

Leprosy

Leprosy creates swelling, discoloration, and numbness in parts of the body. Because it may be spread through contact and was nearly incurable without modern drugs, people with leprosy, called lepers, were often shunned by others and forced to live in remote colonies. The Bible makes many mentions of outcast lepers. In medieval times, lepers would ring a bell as they approached, both as a warning and to ask for charity.

afford to pay slept on the sidewalks and streets, or in public buildings such as railroad stations. Unwanted infants were often abandoned to die on the streets, or left outside clinics and orphanages in the hope that somebody would take them in.

Nearly half the city had no sewer system, and the open drains and gutters smelled foul in the tropical heat. Many families had no place to wash or store food, and some cooked their meals over makeshift fires in the street. Diseases spread quickly in such conditions, especially since homeless people often died on the street. Their bodies could pass on infectious diseases such as tuberculosis, which is spread by coughing and contact, and leprosy, a disease of the skin and nerves that can cause swelling and deformity.

Moti Jihl had all of these problems and more. There was no school or hospital in the area, and garbage was piled next to the smelly drains. It's hard to imagine how the recently uncloistered nun must have felt as she first wandered these filthy streets, or how she maintained her determination when she saw firsthand how enormous the problems that facing her new mission were. She had a list of the families that some of her former students and Sodality members had visited with Father Julien Henry, and stopped to see each of them. At every stop, she explained that she would be starting a school for the neighborhood's children.

The next morning, she returned to Moti Jihl, and was delighted to see that 21 children were waiting for her at the place she had chosen for her school: the steps of a railway bridge next to the muddy pond where their families went every day to get water. She found a spot under a tree and picked up a stick, drawing the letters of the Bengali alphabet

Women and children wait in line for food outside Mother Teresa's mission in Calcutta.

in the mud as the children squatted around her to watch. She had begun her mission, she would say later, "right on the ground."

More children joined her the next day, and still more the next. She was delighted to see how their faces lit up with smiles when she touched their heads or praised them as they recited the alphabet. Soon, Mother Teresa added lessons in hygiene (sometimes giving baths to the dirtier children), catechism, and sewing.

The tiny European nun who dressed like a poor Indian woman soon became a familiar sight to the residents of Moti Jihl, though many were unsure of what she was doing and why. They were not alone: A Jesuit priest named Michael Gabric would later tell an interviewer, "We thought she was cracked." Another priest, disturbed by the example she set for young nuns by going her own way, accused her of following the "wiles of the devil."

As for Mother Teresa herself, her journals from this period (many of which she would later destroy) record her exhaustion and emotional pain at the sights she witnessed every day. Once, she overheard two Hindus saying that her only goal was to convert more people to Christianity. She would later say that the challenges she faced during this time caused her to doubt herself, but she chose to see these doubts as a lesson from God. She was

> ## "We thought she was cracked."
>
> —Father Michael Gabric

determined to put her faith in God's guidance.

As people learned what Mother Teresa was doing, some stepped forward to help with small donations of money or food. When they didn't, she was forced to beg for alms.

People helped Mother Teresa in other ways, too. The bus driver on her route to St. Joseph's Home gave her a free seat beside him. A former teacher from St. Mary's school came to help her teach in her open-air school beneath the tree. A local priest gave her a donation of 100 rupees, enough to rent two small huts. She even had enough money to buy her students milk for lunch every day and bars of soap as prizes. People in the community gave the school furniture and books.

Mother Teresa gave her first lessons to children from Moti Jihl in a makeshift school under a tree.

Two weeks after she started, Mother Teresa had a schoolroom, more than 50 students, and 3 other teachers working alongside her.

The second hut had a sadder purpose. Recently, as she walked through the city streets, Mother Teresa had seen a poor woman dying on the sidewalk. She carried the woman to a nearby hospital, but she was refused entry because she couldn't pay. The woman died on the street. When Mother Teresa spoke of this incident later, she remembered that the dying woman had been most upset by the fact that she was dying alone, forgotten by her family—in fact, she had been very grateful for the compassionate nun's willingness to touch her. Mother Teresa resolved to make a place where the poor could die with dignity and compassionate care.

Father Van Exem continued to meet with Mother Teresa. He was pleased with her progress, but she felt she should leave St. Joseph's Home and strike out on her own. Her efforts to find a new home had met with no success,

A Handful of Rice

Though begging is frowned upon in some Western cultures, giving alms to the poor and to religious figures is a long-standing and honorable tradition in many religions. Buddhist monks make daily rounds with begging bowls, and alms-giving, or *zakat*, is one of the Five Pillars of Islam. In India, a customary donation is a handful of rice.

since landlords refused to rent to a
woman with no source of income.
This gave her added insight into
the plight of the poor she served.
Father Van Exem spoke to a
Bengali Catholic named Albert
Gomes, whose large home
was partially empty, since two
of his brothers had moved to
East Pakistan to work with the
Christian community there. He
invited Mother Teresa to live rent-
free on the second floor.

She moved in with only a suitcase.
Her room was empty except for a chair, a few
wooden boxes, and a painting of the Virgin

Mother Teresa's
mission was right
on the streets.

Mary. At the Gomes home, Mother Teresa would find
additional helpers. Albert's daughter Mabel sometimes went
with her to visit poor families; his brother Michael helped her
obtain donations of medical supplies from local pharmacies.
Charur Ma, a widow who cooked at Loreto Entally,
sometimes joined her on shopping trips and errands. But the
most important help was still to come.

On March 19, 1949, a young girl named Subashini Das
came to the Gomes home. She had been one of Mother
Teresa's students at Loreto Entally, and she wanted to join her
now in her mission to the poorest of the poor.

chapter 9

Three Homes

Subashini Das may have been Mother Teresa's first postulant, but a month later, another of her former Loreto students joined her. By summer, there would be 10 postulants at the Gomes house. Some of these girls had not yet finished high school, and their parents were not always pleased. Mother Teresa worked with them to help them finish their schooling and prepare for their lives as future Missionary Sisters of Charity. The young women went begging from door to door, used the money they got to buy food for the starving, and helped at the children's school and the home for the dying. They lived together and prayed together. But they

Mother Teresa's first group of followers included some of her former students.

had not yet been recognized formally as an order of nuns.

Working from Mother Teresa's original notebooks and lists of rules, Father Van Exem prepared official constitutions for presentation to authorities within the Catho. They were based on the rules of the Sisters of Loreto and the Jesuits, stressing obedience, devotion to the Sacred Heart of Jesus, and a life of poverty. To these basic rules, Mother Teresa added: "Our particular mission is to labor at the salvation and sanctification of the poorest of the poor."

In April 1950, Archbishop Périer took these constitutions with him to Rome, along with photographs of the proposed costumes for postulants (plain white sari over short-sleeved habit), novices (plain white sari over long-sleeved habit), and professed sisters (white sari with blue striped border, as worn by Mother Teresa). Pope Pius XII, then head of the Roman Catholic Church, soon gave his approval to the new order. A small chapel was built on the top floor of the Gomes house, and Archbishop Périer said Mass in it for the first time in October 1950, giving his blessing to the newly formed Missionaries of Charity.

Six months later, the first group of postulants was ready to take their vows as novices. Father Van Exem helped Mother Teresa compose a ceremony in which the

> *"We cannot let a child of God die like an animal in the gutter. . . .*
>
> —Mother Teresa

Indian Wedding Dress

Indian weddings are full of color, joy, and ceremony. The bride is traditionally dressed in an ornately decorated sari in tones of red and gold, wearing gold jewelry on her head, face, and arms. Her hands and feet are elaborately painted with patterns of *henna*, a herbal preparation that makes a long-lasting dye of reddish earth tones.

girls came to the church dressed as Bengali brides (following the "Bride of Christ" tradition of the Catholic Church).

During the service, the postulants withdrew to a room to have their hair cut by Mother Teresa, and reappeared wearing their order's white saris and habits. Since Indian women treasure their glossy black hair, which is traditionally worn long, this represented a huge sacrifice for the young novices. With their heads shorn, returning to a secular life would be difficult, so cutting their hair became a symbol of their commitment to their vocation as Missionary Sisters of Charity.

The new order was growing in other ways, too. By the end of 1952, Mother Teresa had 26 followers, and the living quarters at the Gomes house had become much too crowded. The order was also

SECULAR
Secular means of the world, as opposed to sacred, or of the spirit.

outgrowing the two small huts where
the sisters taught the children of Moti
Jihl and tended the dying. In 1953,
Father Van Exem and Father Julien

MONSOON
The Indian rainy
season is called the
monsoon.

Henry convinced the archdiocese of Calcutta to advance
Mother Teresa enough money to buy a home for the new
order, at 54A Lower Circular Road. This would become
known as the Motherhouse, and it is still the center of
operations for the Missionaries of Charity's work in
Calcutta today.

The Motherhouse was a three-story gray building with
a central courtyard, just off a noisy main road full of cars,
rickshaws, and bicycles. The Missionary Sisters of Charity
owned very little, and what they had was often stretched
thin. At one point, three novices were taking turns wearing
the same pair of sandals. Still others wore habits sewn
from bags that had once contained shipments of bulgur
wheat, sometimes still bearing the stenciled words "Not
For Resale." Their only other
possessions were rosary
beads, an umbrella to protect
them from monsoon rains,
a metal bucket for washing,
and a thin cloth mattress.

There was no room in
the order for disobedience
or questions. Mother Teresa

*"Our particular
mission is to labor
at the salvation
and sanctification
of the poorest of
the poor."*

—Mother Teresa

71

Daily life at the Motherhouse

The rigorous daily schedule of the Missionary Sisters of Charity began at 4:40 AM. After rising, the sisters bathed using water from a tank in the courtyard. They used ash from the stove to brush their teeth, and had one small piece of soap for both their bodies and their clothing. They attended morning prayers, meditation, and Mass, and ate a breakfast of chapati bread, tea or powdered milk, and vitamins. At 7:45, they went into the street in pairs to start work. They returned at noon for prayer, lunch, and rest, then went back to work until 6:00 PM. After a dinner of rice, lentils, and vegetables, they shared their experiences of the day, mended clothes, and went to bed by 10:00.

insisted that every sister ate all that was on her plate, spoke only in English, and shared in the household chores, as she did herself. When one of the novices balked at cleaning the dirty toilet, Mother Teresa got down on her hands and knees and scrubbed it herself, a lesson the girl would never forget. She required not only "total surrender," but "cheerfulness." It was a very hard life, and two of the first ten girls left during their training. Some of the others

were criticized or shunned by family members who were ashamed of their poverty, or simply wished they would finish their schooling or marry.

Along with the Motherhouse, the Missionaries of Charity opened two other houses during these years. The first, provided by the city of Calcutta, was a home for the dying that Mother Teresa called Nirmal Hriday, which meant "Pure Heart" in Bengali. "We cannot let a child of God die like an animal in the gutter," Mother Teresa told journalist Eileen Egan.

The building the city officials offered to her was a large one on the banks of the Hooghly River, a tributary of the sacred Ganges. It was right next to the Temple of Kali, one of the most important Hindu goddesses.

This temple attracted many pilgrims, including some who were ill and wished to die in a sacred

Kali the Dark Mother

Like many Hindu gods and goddesses, Kali takes many forms. Although she is most often represented as a fearsome figure of death, with jet-black skin, four arms, and a necklace of skulls, she is also revered as a mother goddess.

MOTHER TERESA'S HOME OF THE DYING DESTITUTES
NIRMAL HRIDAY
MISSIONARIES OF CHARITY

Nirmal Hriday now bears a sign honoring Mother Teresa and the Missionaries of Charity.

site. Mother Teresa welcomed people of all faiths, but some Hindus were deeply offended by a Christian order opening a home for the dying so close to their temple. It was rumored that the nuns planned to convert people to Catholicism on their deathbeds. Sometimes people threw stones at the sisters, and once a man even threatened to kill Mother Teresa. Another time, a group of protesters entered Nirmal Hriday with a policeman, hoping that he would evict the sisters, but the protesters were so moved by the way the nuns tended the bone-thin, infected bodies of the dying that they changed their minds.

When a Hindu priest suffering from late-stage tuberculosis was turned away by several hospitals, he was brought to Nirmal Hriday, where the Missionary Sisters

of Charity cared for him until he died. After this incident, the tension between the two groups lessened. Pilgrims to the Temple of Kali sometimes stopped at Nirmal Hriday to make donations, and some Hindu women even came to work there as volunteers.

Still, some volunteers were dismayed that the Missionary Sisters of Charity, while ministering tenderly to dying people, did not focus on saving the lives of others with basic medical care and vitamins. After all, the main health problem of many Indians was malnutrition, not deadly disease. For some people with medical backgrounds, such as Dr. Marcus Fernandes, an idealistic young doctor who worked briefly with Mother Teresa at Nirmal Hriday, this was hard to accept.

Sisters tend to the sick and dying in the men's ward of Nirmal Hriday home.

"I Am Going to Heaven Today."

—Inscription on the wall at Nirmal Hriday

The nuns' attitude towards death was summed up by a sign posted high on the wall: "I Am Going to Heaven Today."

Mother Teresa's next project was a home for abandoned babies and children, which she called Shishu Bhavan. In Calcutta, infants were often orphaned, or left to die by desperate parents who couldn't afford to feed them. Sometimes these babies were premature, disabled, or nearly dead from starvation. Some died within hours of arrival at Shishu Bhavan, but Mother Teresa felt very strongly that they should be cared for and held so that they could experience love, even if only for a brief time. As they grew

Mother Teresa quickly overcame her timidity around babies, and developed a special fondness for the young people she helped.

stronger, the healthier babies were given to adoptive parents or sent to boarding schools like Loreto Entally that took in orphans.

As word got out in the community about Mother Teresa's new institution, people started bringing babies to the home from the police stations, hospitals, and schools where they had been abandoned. Mother Teresa made it known that at Shishu Bhavan, no child would ever be refused a bed, even if it meant that three or more had to sleep on one cot. Some

The nuns at Shishu Bhavan often put several babies in the same crib, rather than turn any child away.

of the smallest and frailest babies were kept warm by light bulbs hanging over the cribs and boxes where they slept. Many local residents rallied behind Shishu Bhavan, gathering donations of food, money, clothing, and children's toys. It was to be only the first of many such homes, as the Missionaries of Charity continued to grow.

10

Mother to the World

The movement that had begun when one determined nun walked into the slums grew quickly. More young women came to the Motherhouse wanting to join the new order, and volunteers from many walks of life—doctors, nurses, teachers, and even society wives who wished to do charity work—lent their support.

By 1958, the Missionaries of Charity had established Shishu Bhavan children's homes in several more Calcutta neighborhoods. For older children, Shishu Bhavans established programs to teach skills such as typing, carpentry, and needlework that would help them find jobs. They also sought wealthy sponsors who pledged to pay educational expenses for one or more children, and continued to look for adoptive homes for them. Thanks to Shishu Bhavans, children found homes with Christian and Hindu families in India and with families from Europe and North America as well.

Mother Teresa also started a program of mobile clinics to help people in parts of Calcutta that didn't have access to medical help. In 1956, New York City's Catholic Relief Services donated $5,000 to

DISPENSARY

A dispensary is a charity-run medical clinic where medicines are given away, or dispensed, free of charge.

help the Missionaries of Charity convert an old van into a traveling medical dispensary.

This program took on a new urgency when a hospital for lepers in Gobra closed suddenly, leaving thousands of sufferers with no place to turn. A second van, colored bright blue, was outfitted specially for the treatment of leprosy, and made rounds between eight stations in different parts of the city. A retired physician named Dr. Sen, who specialized in skin diseases, volunteered to oversee this new outreach program. By 1958, more than 600 lepers were receiving regular treatment.

Mother Teresa's mobile dispensary visited neighborhoods whose residents had no access to medical care.

The shelter and services provided by the Missionaries of Charity were sometimes humble, but they were a welcome improvement for many leprosy sufferers.

Lepers were social outcasts in India, and many people who contracted the disfiguring disease were thrown out by frightened and ashamed family members. Unable to work and with no place to live, they had little choice but to become beggars. Wanting to do more for these people, Mother Teresa went to visit a Calcutta suburb called Titlagarh, where a group of lepers had formed a small makeshift village alongside an industrial swamp. Most of them could not afford the train or bus fare to Calcutta to receive services from the mobile van, and even if they could scrape together the money, they were often banned from riding on public transportation.

Mother Teresa resolved to open a new clinic, and sent several Sisters with medical training to work in Titlagarh. She launched a citywide campaign called "Touch a Leper with Your Compassion" to help raise funds. Although the first wave of construction in Titlagarh was met by gangs throwing stones, the sisters soon overcame the community's resistance and opened a hospital, rehabilitation center, and cafeteria. As important as the medicines they dispensed was the sisters' attitude towards these long-suffering people. Instead of avoiding all physical contact, they were happy to touch and comfort the lepers, seeing in their plight the sufferings of Jesus Christ. This went against established medical practice, and Mother Teresa was sometimes criticized for not encouraging her followers to protect themselves by wearing sterile gloves.

The facility for leprosy in Titlagarh was soon followed by a second, called Shantinagar, which means "place of peace." The land for the facility—34 acres of overgrown jungle—was donated by the Indian government. When money ran short during construction, the Sisters of Charity did what they always did: They prayed.

Their prayers were sometimes answered in unexpected ways. In 1964, Pope Paul VI would make an official state visit to India, traveling in a specially imported white Lincoln Continental. He was so impressed by the Nirmal Hriday home for the dying that he gave this car to Mother Teresa when he left India. She immediately raffled it off, raising about $100,000—enough money to finish construction at Shantinagar.

During these years of expansion, Mother Teresa began to realize the value of public relations. She had been the subject of many flattering articles in the Indian press, which had resulted in further donations and new volunteers.

The glittering lights of the Strip in Las Vegas were a startling contrast to the slums of Calcutta.

Starting in 1959, the Missionaries of Charity expanded their operations in India to the cities of Delhi, Jhansi, and Bombay (now called Mumbai). Prime Minister Jawaharlal Nehru attended the opening ceremony of a Shishu Bhavan children's home in the capital city of New Delhi, where he spoke warmly to Mother Teresa about her work.

In the fall of 1960, Mother Teresa set her sights even farther afield. By now, she was 50 years old and in charge of 119 nuns and hundreds of volunteers. In keeping with her increasingly public profile, she accepted an invitation to travel to the United States. Her first stop: a convention of the National Council of Catholic Women in Las Vegas, Nevada.

It's hard to imagine a more unlikely destination for a missionary nun who hadn't traveled outside of India for 30 years. Sometimes known as "The Entertainment Capital of the World," the desert resort also went by the name of "Sin City."

Since the mid-1940s, when gangster Bugsy Siegel established the Flamingo Hotel in the sleepy desert town, Las Vegas had been known for its gambling casinos, liquor, adult entertainment, and connections to organized crime. Its chief attraction was a four-and-a-half-mile (7.2 km) stretch of brightly lit hotels, casinos, and entertainment venues known as the Strip.

When asked what she thought of Las Vegas, Mother Teresa made no mention of its gambling resorts and nightclubs, but replied tactfully that the bright neon lights of the Strip reminded her of the Indian festival of lights, Diwali.

During this trip, Mother Teresa went out to the

Festival of Lights

Diwali is a joyous holiday, celebrated throughout India. A major religious holiday for Hindus, Jains, Sikhs, and Nepali Buddhists, it is also a school holiday and time of family celebration. Diwali is celebrated on the new moon of the Autumn month of Kartika, when celebrants decorate their homes with lights (often rows of small clay oil lamps), set off fireworks, offer prayers to the goddess Lakshmi, and exchange sweets and gifts.

nearby desert to gather spiny thorns from a cactus. When she arrived home in Calcutta, she twisted these into a crown of thorns and placed it on the head of the statue of Christ in the Missionaries of Charity's chapel.

But however exotic the convention's location may have seemed to Mother Teresa, her fund-raising speech was an unqualified triumph. It was her first time onstage as a public speaker, and she addressed the 3,000 Catholic women at the convention in simple, heartfelt terms, talking about her mission among the poorest of the poor. She told them that she had not come to ask for donations, because she believed that God would provide, but invited her audience to look for ways they could do something beautiful for God. Many of them gave her handfuls of cash as they left the auditorium, stuffing the small bag she carried so full that she had to empty it three times into something larger to hold all the money.

Mother Teresa's tour of America continued with stops in Peoria, Illinois; Chicago; and New York City. She had hoped to meet with the newly elected American president John F. Kennedy, who was a practicing Catholic, but this did not come to pass. However, she did meet with the influential radio and television evangelist Bishop Fulton J. Sheen, and with the director of the World Health Organization. Then she continued to Europe.

In London, Mother Teresa met with a representative of Oxfam, an organization that works to alleviate poverty and suffering throughout the world, and was interviewed by the

British Broadcasting Corporation (BBC). A border guard patrols a checkpoint on the Albanian border.

She then continued to Germany, where she was greeted enthusiastically by representatives of the Catholic relief agency Misereor. They pledged their financial support to a planned home for the dying in Delhi, asking only that the Missionaries of Charity send a financial report to show how the money was spent. They were astonished when Mother Teresa refused, saying that her sisters did not have the time or expertise to provide such documents. Her refusal to follow standard accounting procedures would be the source of much controversy as the Missionaries of Charity grew ever larger.

She also made stops in Switzerland and Rome, where she had an emotional reunion with her brother Lazar, the first time she had seen any of her family members since her departure for Ireland at age 18. As an Albanian soldier, Lazar had joined the Italian army during World War II. He and others who served in Italy (an Axis ally of Germany and Japan) were now considered traitors and were forbidden to return home to Albania under threat of death. Although Lazar had made a new life for himself in Italy—where he worked for a company that manufactured medicines, and had an Italian wife and young daughter—he longed to visit his mother and sister, who had moved from Skopje to Albania before World War II broke out. Mother Teresa applied for a visa so that she could visit them herself, but her request was turned down, either because of her brother's military history or because the now-Communist government of Albania did not approve of her affiliation with the Catholic Church.

Mother Teresa eventually went back to India, but even as she returned to her usual work, the world around her was changing. For example, the church itself was undergoing some profound changes during the 1960s. Pope John XXIII convened the Second Vatican Council in 1962, looking for ways to modernize some of the church's ancient rituals. During this period, some texts were changed from Latin to modern languages, certain rules (such as the ban on eating meat on Fridays) were relaxed, and many nuns stopped wearing traditional habits.

There would be no updating of Mother Teresa's order, however. From the start, she had insisted on rigid discipline and unquestioning obedience from her followers, even

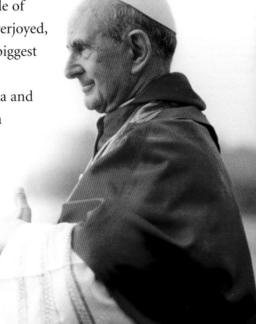

PONTIFICAL

Pontifical means having to do with the pontiff, another name for the pope.

going so far as to give the sisters a specific prayer to recite as they put on each garment. The Missionary Sisters of Charity were forbidden to read newspapers and magazines or listen to radio news, since Mother Teresa felt that awareness of current events would be a distraction from their religious vocation. She also discouraged them from pursuing higher education, with the occasional exception of medical training.

But old-fashioned and sheltered as they may have been, the Missionaries of Charity were about to enter the larger world in a very significant way. In 1965, Pope Paul VI granted permission for Mother Teresa's order to become a Society of Pontifical Right, giving them permission to move outside of India for the first time. Overjoyed, she described this as "the biggest miracle of all."

That July, Mother Teresa and five other sisters boarded a plane to Venezuela, where they were to found their first international home.

Pope Paul VI, who served as pope from 1963 to 1978, helped reform the Catholic church with the Second Vatican Council, which was completed during his papacy.

chapter **11**

A Pencil in God's Hand

The Missionaries of Charity launched its first venture outside of India in the small town of Cocorote, Venezuela. The new environment provided many challenges; the sisters were faced with a new language barrier (locals spoke Spanish and native dialects), unfamiliar customs, and treacherous jungle terrain. Led by Sister Nirmala, a Hindu-born convert, the nuns found themselves doing everything from preparing local children for the rituals of First Communion and Confirmation to repairing roofs in the wake of a tropical storm.

A Missionary Brother of Charity provides medication to an AIDS patient in Port-au-Prince, Haiti.

The home in Venezuela would soon be followed by others on every continent but Antarctica.

This enormous growth created an urgent need for more workers. After consulting Father Van Exem, Mother Teresa asked the Archbishop of Calcutta for permission to create a

male order, called the Missionary Brothers of Charity. Since Catholic law would not allow a woman to oversee a male order, she searched far and wide for a suitable leader. In 1966, Father Ian Travers-Ball, an Australian-born Jesuit, stepped forward to head the Missionary Brothers of Charity, changing his name to Brother Andrew in 1968. The Brothers worked primarily with young boys, offering them free meals and vocational training. Some of the boys went to live in various Missionaries of Charity–run homes in and around Calcutta, where they learned skills such as radio repair or farming.

Like the Missionary Sisters of Charity, the new order grew rapidly, though not without some clashes between Brother Andrew and Mother Teresa. Brother Andrew favored a more informal organizational structure, and wanted the brothers to dress not in clerical garb but in T-shirts and jeans, feeling this would make them more accessible. Eventually he left the order,

and was replaced by Brother Geoff, whose management style was more in line with Mother Teresa's vision.

Mother Teresa also created an organization for lay (unordained) volunteers, borrowing a name Gandhi used for his helpers: Co-Workers. Since the 1950s, many people from all walks of life had helped the Missionaries of Charity in many ways. Doctors, nurses, and dentists often provided free care. There were also a number of British families and officers' wives who had donated time, money, and goods to Mother Teresa's projects while they lived in India. When some of these supporters returned to England, they started new

Mother Teresa was enthusiastically received at the White House by Ronald and Nancy Reagan.

chapters of Co-Workers there. By the 1990s, there were approximately 30,000 volunteer Co-Workers in England, and another 10,000 in other parts of Europe and in the United States. Some of them raised hundreds of thousands of dollars. This money was used to buy bulk supplies such as powdered milk, protein biscuits, and clothing, and to ship them to Missionaries of Charity homes in Africa, Asia, Central America, and South America.

By the late 1960s, Mother Teresa herself had become a more visible figure. Since her first fundraising tour back in 1960, she had appeared on the covers of various Catholic magazines, and word of her work was beginning to reach an international audience. In 1968, the BBC asked noted journalist Malcolm Muggeridge to do a half-hour television interview with a missionary nun. Muggeridge was not enthusiastic at first. He had never heard of Mother Teresa, and found her rather shy and stiff on-camera. "Mother Teresa's answers were perfectly simple and perfectly truthful; so much so that I had some uneasiness about keeping the interview going for the required half hour," he later admitted. "Controversy, the substance of such programmes, does not arise in the case of those who, like Mother Teresa, are blessed with certainties." The footage did not seem in any way extraordinary; there was some question of whether the interview would even be broadcast. But when it aired on the Sunday night series *Meeting Point,* the response from viewers was so overwhelming that the BBC decided to run

it again. Both times, the airings were followed by outpourings of unsolicited donations.

Muggeridge became excited, and asked the BBC to send him to India to make a documentary about Mother Teresa and her followers. The BBC agreed, but Mother Teresa was reluctant at first. Eventually, however, she agreed to give Muggeridge and his cameraman full access for a five-day shoot, "if this TV program is going to help people to love God better." Five days is an absurdly short shooting schedule for a film, but the shoot went without a hitch. Initially, the filmmakers thought they wouldn't be able to film inside Nirmal Hriday, because the only available light, filtering down from high windows, was far too dim. But cameraman Ken Macmillan had a new Kodak film that he wanted to try, so they took some shots anyway. Later, when they reviewed the rushes in London, both men were startled by the clarity and beauty of the Nirmal Hriday footage.

Macmillan said, "You could see every detail. And I said, 'That's amazing. That's extraordinary.' And I was going to go on to say, you know, three cheers for Kodak. I didn't get a chance to say that though, because Malcolm, sitting in the front row, spun round and said: 'It's divine light! It's Mother Teresa.'"

In no time at all, the story of this photographic miracle was picked up by the popular press, and Mother

Teresa had become a media star. Muggeridge's documentary, *Something Beautiful for God*, was followed by a book of the same name, and both were enormously popular. The title came from a letter that Mother Teresa sent Muggeridge shortly after the shoot: "I can't tell you how big a sacrifice it was to accept the making of a film—but I am glad now that I did so because it has brought us all closer to God. In your own way try to make the world conscious that it is never too late to do something beautiful for God." Producer and director Peter Chafer, though not a religious man, declared

The footage of Mother Teresa showed her relaxed and laughing as she spoke about her mission.

Mother Teresa "one of the most extraordinary people I have ever met . . . very practical and running a very tight ship. I think she's awfully good at being a nun."

In time, Mother Teresa would be the subject of several other films, including a 1986 documentary by Emmy Award winners Ann and Jeanette Petrie, and a far more controversial 1994 television film, *Hell's Angel* by Tariq Ali.

With this high visibility came an increase in volunteers, donations, and honors for Mother Teresa. She had already won several major awards in India, always spending the prize money on the Missionaries of Charity's new projects. In 1971, she was awarded the first Pope John XXIII Peace Prize, which came with a check for 10,000 British pounds. During this time, she was also moving her operations into needy neighborhoods in prosperous cities such as London and New York, saying that she was astonished when Westerners wrote checks to help the poor in India, but seemed not to notice the poor and suffering in their own backyards.

Still, Mother Teresa continued to do things in her own way, maintaining that God would provide for her workers as well as for those they served. Many were amazed when she refused an offer from New York's Cardinal Terence Cooke to pay $500 a month to each Sister of Charity working in Harlem, asking him, "Do you think, Your Eminence, that God is going to become bankrupt in New York?"

Mother Teresa had always insisted that her followers live in the same poverty as the people they served. When she considered buildings that were donated too elegant, she had them systematically stripped of such luxuries as carpeting, comfortable mattresses, and even water heaters and radiators. Some people scoffed at the notion of nuns going out of their way to deny themselves comfort, feeling the poor they served would have been glad to be given such things. Years later, the order's refusal to accept a legally

mandated handicapped-access elevator even prevented a new home from opening in New York. Former Missionary Sister of Charity Susan Shields remembers, "Mother would not allow an elevator. The city offered to pay for the elevator. Its offer was refused. After all the negotiations and plans, the project for the poor was abandoned because an elevator for the handicapped was unacceptable."

"It is easy to love the people far away. It is not always easy to love those close to us."

— Mother Teresa

The 1970s also saw one of the Missionaries of Charities' few failures, as a home they opened in violence-ridden Belfast, Ireland, was forced to shut down within 18 months.

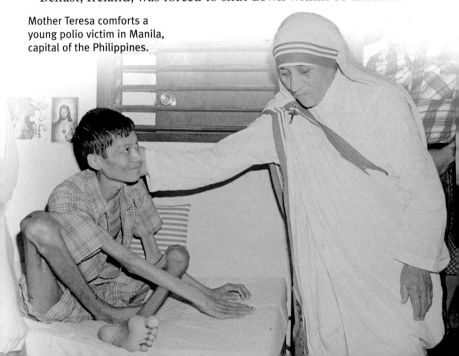

Mother Teresa comforts a young polio victim in Manila, capital of the Philippines.

The Iron Curtain

The "Iron Curtain" was the name given by British Prime Minister Winston Churchill to the symbolic, physical, and military boundaries between Communist-led and Western European countries after World War II. Though the term most often referred to political divisions, there were numerous boundary fences between Communist and democratic nations. The most famous physical barrier, the concrete Berlin Wall which divided the city between East and West Germany, was demolished in 1989.

The Sisters' hasty retreat was never fully explained.

This was also a period of personal tragedy for Mother Teresa. She and Lazar had not forgotten their family, trapped behind the Iron Curtain in Albania. Drana's health was poor, and she had written an emotional letter to Lazar, saying her only wish was to see him and his family, and her daughter Gonxha, before she died. Both Lazar and Mother Teresa made efforts to bring Drana and Aga to Italy, but the Albanian government again refused to let them leave. Mother Teresa then looked into traveling to Albania herself, but learned that she might not be allowed to leave the country again if she did. In 1972, she received word that her mother had died. A year later, Aga was dead as well. These private losses weighed heavily on Mother Teresa's spirits, though she continued to work with seemingly tireless energy.

"It will come only when Jesus thinks it is time."

—Mother Teresa on the Nobel Peace Prize

In December 1975, *Time* magazine ran a cover story on Mother Teresa, as part of an article entitled "Saints Among Us." The suggestion that Mother Teresa was a living saint had already been raised many times, but now it reached millions of readers. Her name was put forward—not once but three times—for the prestigious Nobel Peace Prize. One of her early champions was Malcolm Muggeridge, who lobbied the Norwegian committee on her behalf starting in 1972. She was nominated again by impressive teams of supporters in 1975 and 1977. When the 1977 prize went to a different candidate, Mother Teresa said, "I had a good laugh over the Nobel Prize. It will come only when Jesus thinks it is time."

Throughout all this publicity, Mother Teresa tried to divert the attention from herself to the poor she served, and above all to God, calling herself "a little pencil in God's hands." Maybe so, but that pencil was making quite an imprint on the world.

Time magazine chose an image of Mother Teresa for a 1975 cover story on "living saints."

12

Celebrity in Sandals

The announcement came out in October 1979: After three nominations, the Nobel committee had finally agreed to award the Peace Prize to Mother Teresa.

Congratulations poured in from heads of state, religious leaders, and supporters all over the world, but Mother Teresa's reaction was typically self-effacing. Standing in front of the Motherhouse, she told a mob of international reporters and photographers, "I am unworthy. I accept the prize in the name of the poor. The prize is the recognition of the poor world . . . By serving the poor I am serving Him."

Mother Teresa received the Nobel Peace Prize from John Sanness, Chairman of Norway's Nobel Committee, in 1979.

That same day, an abandoned baby girl was brought to Shishu Bhavan. The sisters named her Shanti, or "peace" in Hindi, in honor of Mother Teresa's Peace Prize.

Two months later, Mother Teresa and two other Sisters of Charity flew to Oslo, Norway, to receive the prize medal and a check for approximately $160,000. She had made a request that the $5,000 traditionally spent on a banquet honoring the recipient be given to the hungry instead, and another $64,000 in donations was added by Norwegian supporters. Winters in Norway are very cold, and Mother Teresa, wearing only a gray cardigan sweater and plain black coat over her sari and sandals, cut quite a figure among the dignitaries in fur hats and coats. It was a lavish ceremony with orchestra music, and giant flower arrangements flanking the stage.

The Nobel Prizes

The Nobel Prizes were founded by wealthy inventor, scientist, and pacifist Alfred Nobel. Since 1901, an international committee has honored people for contributions to medicine, science, economics, literature, and world peace. Peace Prize recipients have included Martin Luther King Jr., the Dalai Lama, Mikhail Gorbachev, Jimmy Carter, Woodrow Wilson, Theodore Roosevelt, and Al Gore.

Many people in the audience were shocked by the contents of Mother Teresa's Nobel Prize acceptance speech. Although the international committee represents people of every possible religious background, with a wide variety of social viewpoints, she chose to speak not only about world poverty, but also against abortion. This position has always been part of Catholic teaching, but it is a highly controversial topic that many felt she would have been wise to avoid. Mother Teresa ran into similar troubles when she advised housewives in overpopulated Egypt to "have lots and lots of children," right after the Egyptian government sponsored a series of films urging families to limit their size. Later, at a giant outdoor mass

Pope John Paul II greets Mother Teresa and another sister who attended Mass in his private chapel.

in Knock, Ireland, she urged the crowd, "Let us promise Our Lady who loves Ireland so much that we will never allow in this country a single abortion. And no contraceptives."

In spite of this controversy, which made headlines all over the world, the Nobel Prize made Mother Teresa a household name, and brought

The Presidential Medal of Freedom is the highest U.S. civilian award. Medals are bestowed once a year by the president of the United States.

international recognition of her work to an even higher level. Major corporations made large-scale donations of goods: A British shoe company donated leather to help lepers make shoes, and other companies sent huge quantities of food and money. Private donations increased as well, as did the number of volunteers and Co-Workers around the world.

Throughout the 1980s and early 1990s, Mother Teresa met with a wide array of religious leaders and heads of state, from South African Archbishop Desmond Tutu to Palestine Liberation Organization Chairman Yasser Arafat and French President Valéry Giscard d'Estaing. U.S. president Ronald Reagan awarded her the Presidential Medal of Freedom, and the United Kingdom's Queen

Elizabeth II made her an honorary member of the Order of Merit. Mother Teresa also befriended England's glamorous Princess Diana, who was later dubbed "the People's Princess" because of her many contributions to charity work at home and abroad. In an interview for *Ladies' Home Journal*, Mother Teresa was quoted as saying of Diana, "Oh, she is like a daughter to me." Diana felt a similar kinship, even flying to Rome to see Mother Teresa when she was ill.

An even stranger pairing occured when Mother Teresa met Irish rock star Bob Geldof, lead singer of the Boomtown Rats. Geldoff had produced an international rock concert called Live Aid to raise money for famine victims in Ethiopia. When he met Mother Teresa for the first time in the airport

"She is like a daughter to me," Mother Teresa said of England's Princess Diana.

Irish rock musician and activist Bob Geldof met Mother Teresa in Addis Ababa, Ethiopia.

at Addis Ababa, Ethiopia, he was struck by how tiny and frail she appeared, by her moral purpose and selflessness, and by how "outrageously brilliant" she was with the international press corps: "There was nothing otherworldly or divine about her. The way she spoke to the journalists showed her to be as deft a manipulator of media as any high-powered American PR expert." Geldof also observed: "She struck me as being the living embodiment of moral good." The press dubbed them "the Saint and the Sinner."

A reporter once asked Mother Teresa how it felt to be called a living saint, as she often was. Her response was characteristic: "Possibly, people see Jesus in me. But we can see Jesus in each other. Holiness is meant for all people."

During these years, Mother Teresa also visited many international trouble spots, including some very dangerous places in the war-torn Middle East.

> *"She struck me as being the living embodiment of moral good."*
> —Bob Geldof

In 1982, between attacks of artillery fire, she took a Red Cross convoy across the bombed-out city of Beirut, Lebanon, to rescue 38 severely disabled and mentally ill children who had been stranded in a mental hospital in West Beirut. Despite the danger and the language barrier, the sisters calmed these terrified children with their loving touch and the warmth of their smiles.

While visiting Rome in 1983, Mother Teresa suffered a major heart attack. She was rushed to the hospital, where she underwent emergency surgery. Determined not to let her health problems slow her down, she continued her international outreach and travels as soon as she had recovered. One of the Missionaries of Charity's new projects involved opening hospices for AIDS patients in New York's Greenwich Village, Washington D.C., and later in San Francisco.

Mother Teresa also went to Bhopal, India, when a poisonous gas leak in an

HOSPICE

A hospice is a place or program that cares for the physical, emotional, and spiritual needs of the dying.

American-owned chemical company killed and injured thousands of innocent people, and to the Soviet Union in the wake of a massive nuclear accident in Chernobyl. She even secured permission for the Missionaries of Charity to work with Armenian earthquake victims in hospitals in Armenia and Moscow, the first religious mission in the Soviet Union since religious orders were banned by its government in 1918.

By the end of the decade, Mother Teresa was traveling up to 10 months of each year, leaving the Motherhouse in others' hands. She preferred to fly coach or travel by train, usually accompanied by at least one other Missionary Sister of Charity. It was a far cry from her humble beginnings on the ground of Moti Jihl. Now Mother Teresa touched thousands of lives as her work spread around the globe.

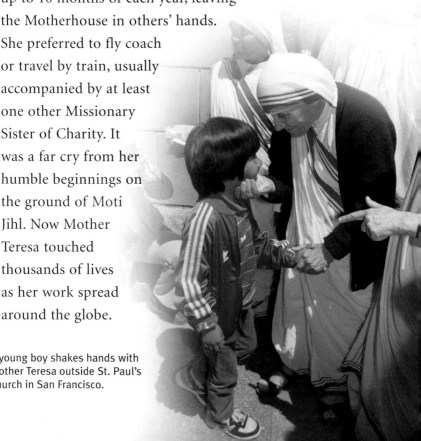

A young boy shakes hands with Mother Teresa outside St. Paul's Church in San Francisco.

chapter 13

Through Doubts and Darkness

In 1988, Mother Teresa met with British media magnate Robert Maxwell, who owned the London tabloid newspaper the *Daily Mirror*. Maxwell, who had already received a lot of negative publicity for his shady business dealings, offered to raise money for a new Missionaries of Charities home in London. Mother Teresa accepted, and posed for newspaper photos with him. Nearly half a million dollars was

Once shy about speaking in public, Mother Teresa became very comfortable with press interviews.

raised from readers of the *Daily Mirror* and the *Scottish Daily Record*, but the money never reached her, or the poor for whom it was intended: It seems likely that Maxwell, who died a few years after the campaign ended, put the funds into his own accounts.

Mother Teresa suffered a second, near-fatal heart attack in 1989. She had extensive surgery and was fitted with a pacemaker, a small electrical device used to regulate the heartbeat. Again, she stubbornly continued to travel and work as soon as she could. Although she made an attempt to resign as the head of the Missionaries of Charity and even spoke to the pope about it, she was reelected by the order and accepted the position without naming a potential successor.

Her role as a media darling was starting to falter along with her health. Although she still received plenty of good press for her charitable work, she was often portrayed not as a living saint, but as a demanding and difficult woman whose saintly reputation protected her from careful scrutiny.

In 1994, British television premiered Tariq Ali's film *Hell's Angel,* which caused tremendous controversy by claiming that Mother Teresa accepted donations from dictators and questioning her priorities in spreading her resources so thinly around the world. The Pakistani producer made the film with the participation of an Indian-born physician, Dr. Aroup Chatterjee, who had long been critical of Mother Teresa's reputation in the West, and an outspoken journalist named Christopher Hitchens.

A physically frail but undaunted Mother Teresa appears in public with her future successor, Sister Nirmala (left), and others.

Two years earlier, Hitchens had published an article in *The Nation* that accused Mother Teresa and her organization of having more interest in spreading Catholic beliefs than in actually helping the poor. After narrating Ali's documentary, Hitchens went on to write a book that detailed Mother Teresa's acceptance of gifts from Robert Maxwell, Haitian dictator Jean-Claude "Baby Doc" Duvalier, and American lawyer and banker Charles Keating, whose savings-and-loan fraud was one of the biggest financial scandals of its time. Hitchens called Mother Teresa, among other things,

"Give Christ to the world, and in doing so, use your hands."

—Mother Teresa

"a religious fundamentalist, a political operative, a primitive sermonizer and an accomplice of worldly, secular powers." His well-researched attack was so savage that certain reviewers dismissed it, and

Mother Teresa's supporters simply maintained that she had no interest in worldly politics. As for Mother Teresa herself, she refused to read the book, but told Hitchens that God forgave him for writing it. (He found this especially infuriating, saying that he neither sought nor wanted forgiveness.)

Less extreme voices also sounded notes of criticism. Dr. Robin Fox, editor of the medical magazine *The Lancet,* wrote about the disorganized approach to the dying at Nirmal Hriday, claiming that the Sisters of Charity used no medical procedures to assess the difference between curable and incurable cases, and caused much suffering by their refusal to offer strong painkillers. Others complained that volunteers were given next to no training, and risked contracting infectious diseases themselves because of Mother Teresa's dictum, "Touch them, wash them, feed them. Give Christ to

Mother Teresa delighted in practicing the Missionaries of Charity principle of caring through human touch.

the world, and in doing so, use your hands." One volunteer wrote of her horror at seeing intravenous needles reused repeatedly at Nirmal Hriday without proper sterilization. When she metioned this, she was told, "There's no point. There's no time." English-born doctor Jack Preger recalled that "tubercular patients were not simply walking among the others, they were eating together and using the same utensils. I begged Mother for a separate ward so that they would not transmit the disease, but it never happened." A small number of volunteers did contract tuberculosis and other illnesses, while others (including a few founding sisters) became disillusioned and left.

Throughout the 1990s, Mother Teresa's own health continued to weaken, though she stubbornly kept working, barely slowing down to recover from each new fall or surgery. In 1997, the Missionaries of Charity finally chose a successor to lead their order. Though the 86-year-old Mother Teresa stayed on as the organization's spiritual head, a younger Indian woman named Sister Nirmala, who had run the Missionaries of Charity's first international home in Cocorote, Venezuela, took over the day-to-day operations. The eldest of 10 children, Nirmala Joshi was born into an upper-caste Hindu family, but converted to Catholicism at age 24 because she was so moved by the Sisters of Charity's work with the poor. "Now I am happy," Mother Teresa announced from the balcony of the Motherhouse. "Pray so she can continue God's work."

However, as the later publication of her private letters to Father Van Exem and other spiritual consultants would show, Mother Teresa was anything but happy during these years. For more than four decades, she had kept a dark secret from the world, a private agony of spiritual despair. The language in her letters is stark and haunting: "Since 49 or 50 this terrible sense of loss—this untold darkness—this loneliness—this continual longing for God—which gives me that pain deep down in my heart—Darkness is such that I really do not see—neither with my mind nor with my reason—The place of God in my soul is blank. There is no God in me—When the pain of longing is so great—I just long and long for God."

Sister Nirmala became the new head of the Missionaries of Charity in 1997.

14

A Modern Saint?

Mother Teresa's spiritual suffering was an entirely private matter, something she hid from all but her closest colleagues as she continued to do what she still called God's work with her characteristic bright smile. "I want only God in my life," she wrote. "'The work' is really and solely His." To some, the fact that she was able to pursue a devoutly religious calling and do good works in spite of her inner darkness was a true test of faith: Even when she could not feel God's presence herself, she never stopped believing in him.

She would soon suffer two more devastating losses, with the deaths of her lifelong friend and

Mother Teresa relied on prayer, writing, and her strong faith to see her through her life's challenges.

mentor Father Van Exem and Princess Diana. Father Van Exem's health had been faltering along with Mother Teresa's, and in a letter to her written shortly before he died, he expressed

his hope that "the Lord may take me and not you if that is His will." She was recovering from heart surgery when that day came, and was too ill to attend his funeral.

Princess Diana had recently gone through a highly publicized divorce, and when she started dating another man, she found herself pursued by reporters and paparazzi wherever she went.

As her date's driver sped through a Paris tunnel to outrun the paparazzi, they swerved to avoid another car and crashed into a column. Diana was killed. This senseless and tragic death was an especially difficult blow for Mother Teresa, and not long afterward, on the eve of Diana's elaborate funeral, she died of a heart attack in the Motherhouse.

A private service was held for her in the Motherhouse chapel, and her body was put into a Missionaries of Charity ambulance with the word "Mother" written on it and driven to St. Thomas Church, where thousands of mourners came to pay their last respects. A week later, the government of India held an official state funeral, full of pomp and circumstance. Mother Teresa's body was

"I want only God in my life."

—Mother Teresa

carried on the same gun carriage that had been used for the funerals of Gandhi and Jawaharlal Nehru, and many thousands lined the streets and packed the stadium where a funeral Mass was held. The service was held in four languages—English, Latin, Bengali, and Hindi—and included addresses by Sister Nirmala and Catholic officials, speeches from representatives of six other major religions, and the singing of hymns. At last, Mother Teresa was laid to rest on the grounds of the Motherhouse, under a plain stone slab.

Almost immediately, the Catholic Church began taking steps towards making Mother Teresa an official saint, setting aside the usual five-year waiting period by order of Pope John Paul II.

Father Brian Kolodiejchuk was selected to head the team investigating Mother Teresa's

The massive crowds that gathered for Mother Teresa's funeral were evidence of her immense celebrity.

The Making of a Saint

In the early centuries of the Catholic church, there were no official guidelines for declaring someone a saint. Starting around 1000 CE, Church officials, and later the pope himself, took responsibility for conferring sainthood. Today, the steps toward sainthood (each of which may take decades) are:

1) Opening of the Cause. A local bishop starts an investigation of the life and work of someone of "extraordinary holiness" who has died, and presents evidence to the Vatican.

2) A postulator examines this evidence and the claims of miracles attributed to the candidate.

3) The candidate is beatified if a miracle is verified, of if he or she is a martyr (someone who died for his or her religious beliefs).

4) If a second miracle is verified, the candidate can be canonized, or made a saint.

proposed sainthood. The team put together 67 volumes of evidence and held tribunals all over the world, hearing testimony from hundreds of witnesses. Nearly all supported Mother Teresa's bid for sainthood, saying that she had met the traditional virtues of faith, hope, charity, prudence, justice, fortitude, and temperance. Three non-Catholics gave testimony against her, including Christopher Hitchens, who quipped that he had been placed in the traditional "devil's advocate" role.

Several alleged miracles were examined by the team, including one experienced by a Hindu woman named Monika Besra who had come to the Sisters of Charity suffering from a stomach tumor after Mother Teresa's death. She claimed the tumor disappeared when the Sisters prayed to Mother Teresa and held a religious medal that had been touched by Mother Teresa against Besra's belly. There are numerous other claims of posthumous miracles, but none has yet been accepted by church authorities.

On October 19, 2003, six years after Mother Teresa's death, Pope John Paul II celebrated his 25th year as pope by announcing her beatification. This was the shortest waiting period in the history of the church for someone to be beatified.

Fireworks explode over Vatican City in celebration of Mother Teresa's beatification.

A wide variety of Mother Teresa memorabilia is for sale at souvenir stands in Vatican City.

The simple nun from Skopje would now be known as Blessed Mother Teresa of Calcutta (now usually spelled Kolkata).

The beatification ceremony in Vatican City was accompanied by a media frenzy and a flood of Mother Teresa merchandise. The Vatican issued a commemorative stamp, and factories churned out thousands of rosaries, medals, key chains, and other religious souvenirs: One gift shop offered life-size fiberglass statues at $1,650 each. The Missionaries of Charity even took the step of trademarking Mother Teresa's name and the order's name and logo to protect them from commercial exploitation.

The Vatican also sponsored a film festival, showing Malcolm Muggeridge's *Something Beautiful for God,* Ann and Jeannette Petrie's *Mother Teresa,* and several other films by directors from around the world. Tariq Ali's controversial *Hell's Angel* was also put on the festival program, but not surprisingly, it was never shown.

Mother Teresa has also been featured on the A&E series *Biography* and as the subject of several dramatic films. She has been played by actresses Geraldine Chaplin and Olivia Hussey, and in 2006, Indian director T. Rajeevnath raised

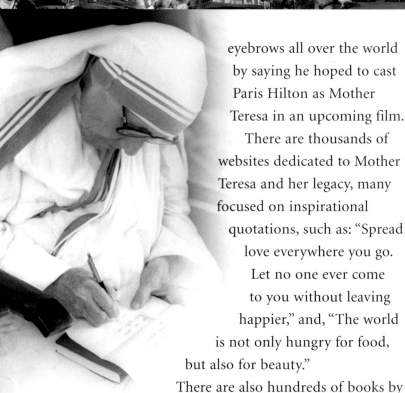

eyebrows all over the world by saying he hoped to cast Paris Hilton as Mother Teresa in an upcoming film. There are thousands of websites dedicated to Mother Teresa and her legacy, many focused on inspirational quotations, such as: "Spread love everywhere you go. Let no one ever come to you without leaving happier," and, "The world is not only hungry for food, but also for beauty."

Mother Teresa's prolific writings continue to inspire.

There are also hundreds of books by and about Mother Teresa. She was credited as the author or coauthor of several books during her lifetime, and more were published after her death. The titles include *A Simple Path, Everything Starts from Prayer, In My Own Words, The Joy in Loving: A Guide to Daily Living, Thirsting For God,* and the recent best seller, edited by Father Brian Kolodiejchuk, *Come Be My Light: the Private Writings of the Saint of Calcutta.* This last book was the first to reveal her many years of spiritual darkness and. Predictably, it has caused a great deal of controversy—not only because of its contents, but because many feel it was

wrong to disobey Mother Teresa's wishes to have these private letters destroyed.

"We must grow in love and to do this we must go on loving and loving and giving and giving until it hurts–the way Jesus did. Do ordinary things with extraordinary love: little things like caring for the sick and the homeless, the lonely and the unwanted, washing and cleaning for them. You must give what will cost you something. This, then, is giving not just what you can live without but what you can't live without or don't want to live without, something you really like. Then your gift becomes a sacrifice, which will have value before God. Any sacrifice is useful if it is done out of love.

This giving until it hurts–this sacrifice–is also what I call love in action.

–Mother Teresa, *A Simple Path*

Today, more than 4,800 Missionary Sisters of Charity, about 400 Brothers, and thousands of volunteers continue Mother Teresa's work in Calcutta and around the world. She continues to evoke a wide variety of responses, as some are more swayed

> *"The world is not only hungry for food, but also for beauty."*
> —Mother Teresa

The Missionaries of Charity organization continues to grow and attract new followers.

by the controversies of her later years, while others consider her a saint, plain and simple.

In the end, it may be Mother Teresa's own words that help separate what she was from what she was not. She was once asked to describe the Missionaries of Charity and what they did, and replied, "We are first of all religious; we are not social workers, not teachers, not nurses or doctors, we are religious sisters. We serve Jesus in the poor."

Though some would take her to task for not providing adequate medical care, or failing to solve the social and political problems that forced the people she served to live in such poverty, Mother Teresa never pretended to be anything but what she was: a religious worker who reached out with her own two hands to spread God's love, and provide what comfort she could to those who had no one to care for them. If she was stubborn and difficult, she was also tremendously disciplined and

> *"Do ordinary things with extraordinary love."*
> — Mother Teresa

effective at what she set out to do. It is hard to overestimate the courage it took for a nun to step outside the traditions of the church to which she had dedicated her life and walk alone into the slums of Calcutta, with no idea whether anyone else would follow in her footsteps. Thousands have, and without question many thousands of lives have been saved and otherwise touched by the order she founded.

This, then, is Mother Teresa's true legacy. By living her life in the way she did, she offered the world an example of just how much difference one person can make through "love in action."

Mother Teresa's mission to help "the poorest of the poor" continues in India and throughout the world.

Events in the Life of Mother Teresa

September 10, 1946
Mother Teresa receives "the call within a call" on the train to Darjeeling; this is later called "Inspiration Day."

January 6, 1929
Agnes arrives in India.

August 15, 1947
British rule over India ends, dividing the former colony into the independent nations of India, Pakistan, and Ceylon.

August 29, 1910
Agnes Gonxha Bojaxhiu is born in Skopje.

1919
Agnes's father, Nikola Bojaxhiu, dies.

May 24, 1931
Agnes takes her first vows, adopting the name Sister Teresa.

November 29, 1928
Agnes leaves home for the Loreto Sisters convent in Ireland.

May 24, 1937
After taking her final vows, Sister Teresa becomes known as Mother Teresa.

April 12, 1947
Pope Pius XII grants Mother Teresa permission to leave the Loreto convent and work with the poor in Calcutta.

January 30, 1948
Gandhi is assassinated.

October 16, 1979
Mother Teresa is awarded the Nobel Peace Prize. She travels to Oslo, Norway, for the award ceremony on December 10.

March 1949
Former student Subashini Das becomes Mother Teresa's first follower.

September 23, 1955
Mother Teresa opens the first Shishu Bhavan home for abandoned babies and children.

March 13, 1997
Sister Nirmala is elected head of Missionaries of Charity.

October 7, 1950
The new order of Missionaries of Charity is formally approved.

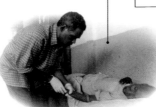

July 12, 1972
Drana Bojaxhiu, Mother Teresa's mother, dies in Tirana, Albania.

August 22, 1952
Mother Teresa opens the Nirmal Hriday home for the dying.

July 26, 1965
Missionaries of Charity opens its first home outside India, in Cocorote, Venezuela.

September 5, 1997
Mother Teresa dies of a heart attack in Calcutta, India.

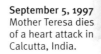

Bibliography

BOOKS:

Egan, Eileen. *Such a Vision of the Street.* Sidewick & Jackson, 1985.

Greene, Meg. *Mother Teresa, a Biography.* Greenwood Press, 2004.

Hitchens, Christopher. *The Missionary Position: Mother Teresa in Theory and Practice.* Verso Books, 1995.

Hurley, Joanna. *Mother Teresa: A Pictorial Biography.* Courage Books/Running Press, 1997.

Kolodiejchuk, Brian, ed. *Mother Teresa: Come Be My Light.* Doubleday, 2007.

Le Joly, Edward. *Mother Teresa of Calcutta: A Biography.* Harper & Row, 1989.

Mattern, Joanne. *Princess Diana.* DK Publishing, 2006.

Mother Teresa Heart of Joy: The Transforming Power of Self-Giving. Servant Books, 1987.

Mother Teresa, compiled by Varney, Lucinda. *A Simple Path.* Ballantine Books, 1995.

Pastan, Amy. *Gandhi.* DK Publishing, 2006.

Royle, Roger & Woods, Gary. *Mother Teresa: A Life in Pictures.* HarperSanFrancisco, 1992.

Sebba, Anne. *Mother Teresa: Beyond the Image* (Updated and Expanded). Image Books, Doubleday, 1998.

Spink, Kathryn. *Mother Teresa: A Complete Authorized Biography.* HarperCollins, 1997.

St. Ignatius Loyola. *The Spiritual Exercises of St. Ignatius Loyola.* Tan Books, 1999.

PERIODICALS AND WEBSITES:

Lattin, Don, "Mother Teresa Gets Fast Track to Sainthood," *San Francisco Chronicle,* 10/12/03.

"Saints Among Us," *Time* magazine cover story, 12/29/75.

Van Biema, David, "Her Agony," *Time* magazine cover story, 9/3/07.

www.brainyquote.com
www.motherteresaawards.com
www.nobelprize.org

DVD AND VIDEO:
Something Beautiful for God BBC Films, directed by Peter Chafer, with Malcolm Muggeridge, 1969

Mother Teresa, Petrie Productions, directed & produced by Ann & Jeannette Petrie, 1986

* The writings of Mother Teresa of Calcutta are copyright by The Mother Teresa Center, exclusive licensee throughout the world of the Missionaries of Charity for the works of Mother Teresa.

Works Cited

CHAPTER 1:
"When you do good, do it quietly..." *Mother Teresa: A Complete Authorized Biography,* p.7

CHAPTER 2:
"Home is where the mother is." *Mother Teresa: A Complete Authorized Biography,* p.6
"What have I done for Christ?" *The Spiritual Exercises of St. Ignatius Loyola*
"You think you are important..." *Mother Teresa: A Complete Authorized Biography,* p.11

CHAPTER 3:
"Thanks be to God, we began the new year well..." *Mother Teresa: A Complete Authorized Biography,* p.13

CHAPTER 4:
"Day and night they live in the open…" *Mother Teresa: Beyond the Image,* p. 33
"If our people could only see this..." *Mother Teresa: Beyond the Image,* p.33
"Each morning, before I start work..." *Mother Teresa: Beyond the Image,* p.34

CHAPTER 5:
"It was very squalid..." *Mother Teresa: Beyond the Image,* p.39
"Dear child, Do not forget..." *Mother Teresa: A Complete Authorized Biography,* p.19
"I saw bodies..." *Such a Vision of the Street,* quoted in *Mother Teresa: A Life in Pictures,* p.23

CHAPTER 6:

"I was sure it was God's voice..." *Mother Teresa: Beyond the Image,* p.46

"Mother was not an exceptional person..." *Mother Teresa: Beyond the Image,* p. 47

"Since this is manifestly the will of God..." *Mother Teresa, a Biography,* p.30

"Can I go to the slums now?" *Mother Teresa, a Biography,* p.33

CHAPTER 7:

"We young ones essentially could not fathom..." *Mother Teresa: A Complete Authorized Biography,* p.31

"Do not criticize..." *Mother Teresa: A Complete Authorized Biography,* p.31

"But Father, I am here." *Mother Teresa: A Complete Authorized Biography,* p.33

CHAPTER 8:

"I am prepared to die..." Mohandas Gandhi, www.brainyquote.com

"...right on the ground," *Such a Vision of the Street,* p.43

"We thought she was cracked." *Such a Vision of the Street,* p.43

"...the wiles of the devil," *Mother Teresa: A Complete Authorized Biography,* p.40

CHAPTER 9:

"Our particular mission is to labor..." *Mother Teresa of Calcutta: A Biography,* p.28

"...total surrender" *Mother Teresa: A Complete Authorized Biography,* p.40

"We cannot let a child of God die..." *Mother Teresa: A Life in Pictures,* p.22

CHAPTER 10:

"...the biggest miracle of all." *Something Beautiful for God,* BBC documentary

CHAPTER 11:

"Mother Teresa's answers were perfectly simple." *Mother Teresa: Beyond the Image,* p.81

"...if this TV program is going to help people love better." *Mother Teresa: Beyond the Image,* p.82

"You could see every detail..." *The Missionary Position,* p. 26

"I can't tell you how big a sacrifice..." *Mother Teresa: Beyond the Image,* p.84

"...one of the most extraordinary people" *Mother Teresa: Beyond the Image,* p.85

"Do you think, Your Eminence..." *Mother Teresa: A Complete Authorized Biography,* p.93

"Mother would not allow an elevator." *The Missionary Position,* p. 45

"I had a good laugh over the Nobel Prize..." *Mother Teresa: Beyond the Image,* p.99

"...a pencil in God's hand," *Mother Teresa: Come Be My Light,* p.xi

CHAPTER 12:

"I am unworthy..." *Mother Teresa: Beyond the Image,* p.100

"...have lots and lots of children," *Mother Teresa: Beyond the Image,* p.111

"Let us praise Our Lady who loves Ireland..." *The Missionary Position,* p. 58

"Oh, she is like a daughter to me." *Ladies Home Journal* interview, quoted in Mother Teresa: Beyond the Image, p.245

"There was nothing otherworldly or divine..." *Mother Teresa: Beyond the Image,* p.115

"She struck me as being the living embodiment..." *Mother Teresa: Beyond the Image,* p.115

"Possibly, people see Jesus in me." *San Francisco Chronicle,* 10/12/03

CHAPTER 13:

"...a religious fundamentalist, a political operative" *The Missionary Position,* p. 11

"Touch them, wash them, feed them..." *Mother Teresa: Beyond the Image,* p.157

"There's no point. There's no time." *The Missionary Position,* p.40

"...tubercular patients were not simply walking" *Mother Teresa: Beyond the Image,* p.148

"Now I am happy..." *Mother Teresa: A Pictorial Biography,* p. 116

"Since 49 or 50 this terrible sense of loss..." *Come Be My Light,* p.210

CHAPTER 14:

"I want only God in my life." *Come Be My Light,* p. 211

"...the Lord may take me..." *Mother Teresa: A Complete Authorized Biography,* p.270

"Spread love everywhere you go." www.brainyquote.com

"The world is not only hungry..." www.motherteresaawards.com

"We must grow in love..." *A Simple Path,* p.87

"We are first of all religious..." *Mother Teresa, a Biography,* p. 139

Index

For Further Study

Browse tributes to Mother Teresa at CNN, www.cnn.com/WORLD/9709/mother.teresa and the Global Catholic Network, www.ewtn.com/motherteresa/

Find more links to online articles about Mother Teresa in the Biography Research Guide, www.123exp-biographies.com/t/00034171398/

Learn more about Mother Teresa and other Nobel Peace Prize recipients at www.nobelprize.org/nobel_prizes/peace/laureates

Abroad, visit the Mother Teresa Memorial Room, park, and fountain in Skopje, Macedonia. A plaque where her house once stood is engraved with her birthdate and the message, "The world is hungry not for bread, but for love."

Acknowledgments

Grateful thanks to Susan Cohen, Sonia Pabley, and Phyllis Wender at the Gersh Agency; to the staff of the Stone Ridge Library; to David Van Biema; to Heidi Hill for her expert eyes; and to my daughter Sophia for her love in action.

Picture Credits

The photographs in this book are used with permission and through the courtesy of:

GETTY IMAGES: pp.1, 59, 97 Time & Life Pictures; pp.7, 13, 122TL Walter Bibikow; p.41 Getty Images; pp.87, 111 AFP

PHOTOFEST: pp. 3, 93

CORBIS: pp.5, 8, 19, 82, 95, 100, 101 Bettman; p.9 The Gallery Collection; p.10 Ethel Davies/Robert Harding World Imagery; p.11 Javier Echezapreta/epa; pp.14, 15, 20, 42 Hulton-Deutsch Collection; p.17 Jacques Pavlovsky/Sygma; pp.25, 122TC Harald Lange/zefa; p.31 Robert Harding World Imagery; p.46 Origlia Franco/Sygma; pp.48-49 John Harper; p.50 Fly Fernandez/zefa; p.52 Peter Adams; p.53 Gary Houlder; p.58 Kamal Kishore/Reuters; p.60 Bradley Smith; pp.63, 115, 123BR Patrick Robert/Sygma; p.72 Jayanta Shaw; p.75 Kapoor Baldev/Sygma; pp.76, 123TC, 124-125, 126-127 Nik Wheeler; p.83 Bob Krist; p.85 Michael Setboun; p.90 Corbis; p.96 Peter Turnley; p.102 Mike Segar/Reuters; p.106 Philip Gould; p.116 Max Rossi/Reuters; p.117 Jon Hicks

ALAMY: pp.6, 55 Tim Graham; pp.22-23, 122BL Profimedia International s.r.o.; p.26 John James; p.29 The Print Collector; p.30 Richard Wareham Fotografie; pp.32, 49T, 99, 114 Mary Evans Picture Library; p.38L Gary Curtis; p.62 Marco Brivio; p.66 Simon Rawles; pp.74, 123BL Lee Karen Stow; p.77 Terry Fincher.Photo.Int

DORLING KINDERSLEY: pp.12, 54

DINODIA: pp.28, 34, 37, 38R, 39, 44, 57, 65, 67, 70, 73, 108, 109, 112, 118, 120, 122TL, 122BR, 123TL

ASSOCIATED PRESS: pp.68, 80, 88, 98, 103, 105, 121, 123TR, 123BC

THE IMAGE WORKS: p.78 Topham

BORDER IMAGES, from left to right:
Photofest; Getty Images/Walter Bibikow; Alamy/Richard Wareham Fotografie; Dinodia; Alamy/Lee Karen Stow; Getty/Tim Graham; Alamy/Tim Graham; Alamy/Profimedia International s.r.o.; Dinodia; Getty Images/Time and Life Pictures; Alamy/Terry Fincher.PhotoInt; The Image Works/Topham; Getty Images; Dinodia; Dinodia; Getty Images/AFP; Photofest

About the Author

Maya Gold is the author of *Harriet the Spy, Double Agent,* a sequel to Louise Fitzhugh's young-adult classic. She is also a television writer, playwright, and magazine journalist. She lives in the Catskill Mountains of upstate New York with her 13-year-old daughter.

Other DK Biographies you'll enjoy:

Marie Curie
Vicki Cobb
ISBN 978-0-7566-1496-6 paperback
ISBN 978-0-7566-1495-9 hardcover

Charles Darwin
David C. King
ISBN 978-0-7566-2554-2 paperback
ISBN 978-0-7566-2555-9 hardcover

Princess Diana
Joanne Mattern
ISBN 978-0-7566-1614-4 paperback
ISBN 978-0-7566-1613-7 hardcover

Amelia Earhart
Tanya Lee Stone
ISBN 978-0-7566-2552-8 paperback
ISBN 978-0-7566-2553-5 hardcover

Albert Einstein
Frieda Wishinsky
ISBN 978-0-7566-1247-4 paperback
ISBN 978-0-7566-1248-1 hardcover

Benjamin Franklin
Stephen Krensky
ISBN 978-0-7566-3528-2 paperback
ISBN 978-0-7566-3529-9 hardcover

Gandhi
Amy Pastan
ISBN 978-0-7566-2111-7 paperback
ISBN 978-0-7566-2112-4 hardcover

Harry Houdini
Vicki Cobb
ISBN 978-0-7566-1245-0 paperback
ISBN 978-0-7566-1246-7 hardcover

Helen Keller
Leslie Garrett
ISBN 978-0-7566-0339-7 paperback
ISBN 978-0-7566-0488-2 hardcover

John F. Kennedy
Howard S. Kaplan
ISBN 978-0-7566-0340-3 paperback
ISBN 978-0-7566-0489-9 hardcover

Martin Luther King, Jr.
Amy Pastan
ISBN 978-0-7566-0342-7 paperback
ISBN 978-0-7566-0491-2 hardcover

Abraham Lincoln
Tanya Lee Stone
ISBN 978-0-7566-0834-7 paperback
ISBN 978-0-7566-0833-0 hardcover

Nelson Mandela
Lenny Hort & Laaren Brown
ISBN 978-0-7566-2109-4 paperback
ISBN 978-0-7566-2110-0 hardcover

Annie Oakley
Chuck Wills
ISBN 978-0-7566-2997-7 paperback
ISBN 978-0-7566-2986-1 hardcover

Pelé
Jim Buckley
ISBN 978-0-7566-2987-8 paperback
ISBN 978-0-7566-2996-0 hardcover

Eleanor Roosevelt
Kem Knapp Sawyer
ISBN 978-0-7566-1496-6 paperback
ISBN 978-0-7566-1495-9 hardcover

Mother Teresa
Maya Gold
ISBN 978-0-7566-0835-4 paperback
ISBN 978-0-7566-0832-3 hardcover

George Washington
Lenny Hort
ISBN 978-0-7566-0835-4 paperback
ISBN 978-0-7566-0832-3 hardcover

Look what the critics are saying about DK Biography!

"…highly readable, worthwhile overviews for young people…" —*Booklist*

"This new series from the inimitable DK Publishing brings together the usual brilliant photography with a historian's approach to biography subjects." —*Ingram Library Services*